About the Author

Joe Peters was just five years old when he watched his beloved father burn to death. The scene struck Joe dumb, literally, and he had no voice for over four years. Left at the mercy of his violent family and unable to ask anyone for help, his life turned into a living hell.

Joe's story casts light into the darkest of hidden worlds, and is the truly inspirational tale of how one small boy found the strength to overcome almost impossible odds and become a remarkable man.

Joe now lives with his wife and soulmate Michelle and their five children. He has set up an internet service to help children like himself and is a spokesman on behalf of all abused children.

Cry Silent Tears

The heartbreaking survival story
of a small mute boy who
overcame unbearable
suffering and found
his voice again

JOE PETERS
with Andrew Crofts

HarperElement
An Imprint of HarperCollins*Publishers* ·
77–85 Fulham Palace Road,
Hammersmith, London W6 8JB

The website address is: www.thorsonselement.com

and *HarperElement* are trademarks
of HarperCollins*Publishers* Ltd

First published by HarperElement 2008
This edition 2008

10 9 8 7 6 5 4 3 2

A catalogue record of this book is
available from the British Library

ISBN-13 978-0-00-727406-2
ISBN-10 0-00-727406-8

Mixed Sources
Product group from well-managed
forests and other controlled sources
www.fsc.org Cert no. SW-COC-1806
© 1996 Forest Stewardship Council
FSC

To Michelle, my soulmate, and my five beautiful
and special children, Darren, Liam, Kirsty-Lea,
Shannon and Paige.

Thanks guys, for all your love and support.
Love Dad.

In Memory of My Dad, "George William"

I hope you are proud of me coming to terms with
the years of pain that I suffered, and hope you can
rest in peace knowing I am safe.

Love, your son (JPx)

Acknowledgements

To Andrew Crofts for helping me organise my chapters and being supportive throughout.

Chapter One

Tug of War

I never doubted for a moment that my dad loved me more than anything or anyone else in the world, and I returned that adoration wholeheartedly from the first moment that I was able to. He was a tall, handsome man with sparkly eyes, who was popular wherever he went, and he made me feel like king of the world every second we were together. I was his first child, his pride and joy, and he put me on as high a pedestal as I put him. 'My little Joe,' he'd say fondly, sitting me on his knee and ruffling my curly brown hair.

In almost all of my early memories, I am clinging to his big long legs, viewing the world from between them, or sitting in his car or on a grass verge nearby watching him while he worked. He was employed as a mechanic for an Irish guy called Graeme who owned a garage in Norwich, and had been with him since he was an apprentice, straight out of school. Graeme's whole family had taken to him as though he was one of their own children and he had repaid their faith in him a hundredfold. He had gradually been given more and more responsibility and trust until he was virtually running the place if Graeme wasn't there and they all thought the world of him. Dad seemed to have that effect on everyone, and I was able to bask in his reflected glory whenever I was with him. I felt safe and happy when he was around.

My mum, on the other hand, was a terrifying woman. She was almost as tall as Dad, with jet-black hair and a scowling face. It seemed to me she was always angry and, in particular, she seemed to be constantly furious with Dad and me. My three older brothers (from her first marriage) got off lightly, but whenever I was near she would lash out, hitting me round the head, kicking me or pushing me over. She called me all kinds of names I didn't understand and screamed at me till I cowered, petrified, in a corner.

Well aware of her violent nature and her hatred for me, Dad kept a watchful eye on me from dawn till dusk. Everywhere he went, I went. As a toddler, I was hardly ever allowed out of his sight. Not only did he take me to work, but he even took me to the toilet with him. Not that I needed much encouragement; I wanted to be as close to him as possible. We were mutually bonded and he took pleasure in indulging my every whim. If I wanted Sugar Puffs he would buy me a box a day and let me eat my way through them. Mum would freak out when she found out.

'You're spoiling him,' she would scream. 'And you're undermining me when I tell him he can't have things.'

'He can have whatever he wants,' Dad would tell her, in a tone that implied that was the end of the discussion.

In my early years, I had no idea why there was this constant raging battle over me, but so long as I could be with Dad that was fine. And when we began to stay at his friend Marie's house instead of with Mum, I was even happier. Marie was pretty and gentle, with long, reddish hair, and she was very nice to me. I liked the way she talked to me, explaining things at a level that I could understand and always taking my feelings into account. In all the years I knew her, I don't think I ever heard her raise her voice. But once we were staying at Marie's, Mum got even more angry and would come round at all hours trying to force Dad to hand me over to her. That used to terrify me and I'd cling to him like a limpet while they shouted at each other.

One day, when I was four, Dad wasn't able to take me to work with him for some reason so he left me with his sister, Melissa, instructing her that on no account was she to let Mum get hold of me. Somehow Mum got to hear about where I was and turned up at Aunt Melissa's house, insisting that she was taking me home with her. Melissa put up a battle but Mum wasn't having any of it. I stood in the hall trembling as the two women screamed abuse at each other, insults flying.

'He's not your fucking child,' Mum yelled. 'I'll call the police and have you done for kidnapping, you fucking cow.'

'You're an unfit mother,' Melissa replied. 'Look at you – half cut at eleven in the morning. Let's see what the police think about that.'

I pressed my hands over my ears to block out the shouting and the next thing I knew, Mum had grabbed one of my arms and dragged me past Melissa out into the street.

'You bitch!' Melissa was screaming, but she let Mum take me. Maybe she felt she had no choice because she wasn't my parent. I was crying out 'No, Mum, no!' as she hauled me down the street, utterly petrified, knowing that I was about to get punished although I had no idea what for.

As soon as we got in the door of Mum's house, she punched me full in the face, sending me hurtling to the floor. She grabbed me by the hair to pull me up again then started beating me round my face and body in a fury. I was screaming at the top of my lungs, twisting away from her but unable to protect myself from the blows that were raining down.

'Shut up, you little bastard,' she hissed. Holding me by the hair, she picked me up and swung me round so that my legs clattered off the wall. When she dropped me, I crumpled to the floor, dazed and half-unconscious from the beating.

Mum wasn't finished though. She looked around the room for some way to punish me that I would never forget and her eye alighted on a hot iron, which was standing on the ironing board. She must have been ironing when she got the call to say I was at Melissa's and she'd left the iron on when she hurried out of the house. She grabbed my hand and yanked me across the room, then pressed my palm tightly against the scalding metal until my flesh sizzled. I screamed uncontrollably with the shock of this unbelievable new level of pain.

'You are a spoiled little bastard,' Mum sneered, 'and you are never going to see your fucking father again.'

She pushed me and I collapsed on the floor, sobbing, clutching my scorched, throbbing hand, terrified that somehow she would manage to arrange things so that I really wouldn't see Dad again. 'Dad,' I sobbed. 'Dad, help me.'

The moment Mum had snatched me from her house, Aunt Melissa had rung Dad in a panic to tell him what had happened. He must have downed tools at the garage and come running immediately but by the time he got to Mum's house he found me in hysterical tears with a black eye and livid burn marks on my hand. As soon as I saw him I ran behind his legs, clinging on with my undamaged hand, shaking with fear, desperate to get away from her.

'Look what you're doing to him!' Dad shouted. 'He's terrified of his own mother.'

'It's not me, it's you,' she screamed back. 'You and your whore! You've turned him against me!'

'What the fuck has he done to his hand?' Dad demanded, looking in horror at the bright-red, blistered skin.

'Oh, he touched the iron,' she lied. 'He was messing around as usual.'

'And what about the bruises on his face?'

'He fell over.'

'Get me out of here, Dad,' I begged. 'Please.'

Mum grabbed one of my arms so Dad quickly grabbed the other one and they both pulled at me, like dogs fighting over an old bone. I thought my arms were going to pop out of their sockets, they pulled so hard. Beside himself with rage Dad punched her in order to force her to let go of me. The moment she released her grip he swept me up into his arms and ran from the house, clutching me to him as if he was never going to let me go. I just screamed and sobbed hysterically. He bundled me into his Ford Capri and drove me to the burns unit at the hospital to have my wounds dressed. I remember I couldn't stop shaking, even after the nurses had given me something to help with the pain. I must have been in shock, I suppose.

'That's it,' Dad told Marie in a grim voice once we were safely back at her house again. 'I'm not leaving him with anyone else; not you, not Melissa, no one. He's going everywhere with me from now on.'

I felt a huge wave of relief. Dad would look after me. He would keep Mum away from me. I would be all right now.

It was soon after this event that Marie sat me down and explained to me about the root of the problems between Mum and Dad. First of all, she told me that Mum (whose name was Lesley) came from a very strict family. Her father was in the army and her mother, a factory worker, had been a strict disciplinarian at home, so Mum must have thought it was normal to bully and beat up children. Maybe she thought that was how all children were brought up.

As Marie spoke, I remembered the times I'd visited my grandmother's house with my older brothers. It felt more like being drilled on an army parade ground than welcomed into a family; everything was forbidden, everything was punishable. If any of us so much as moved we broke some rule or other and ended up being shouted at or slapped. The seeds of violence that were later to grow so strong in Mum must have been sown during the beatings she received from her own mother.

I can't remember how Marie explained the complex relationship between my parents and her to a four-year-old boy. Maybe she just said 'Your mum's cross because your dad wants to stay with me and not her.' But over the years I pieced together their story from bits of information I picked up here and there.

Mum had been married in her teens to her school sweetheart; she was forced by the family to marry after she fell pregnant. Their son, Wally, was to be the first of the three children the young couple would have together, followed over the next few years by two more boys, Larry and Barry. Once she had started having children Lesley became a full-time housewife, an undertaking that would soon become more of an obsession than a lifestyle. Her house was always kept spotless and woe betide anyone who so much as dropped a crumb on a carpet.

From what I've been told the marriage was pretty strong to start with, although the children were all brought up with the same ferocious strictness that Lesley had experienced herself, but the death of their fourth child at birth caused a rift between her and her first husband. The marriage quickly degenerated from that point and ended in divorce, leaving Lesley bringing up three children on her own, feeling angry and resentful towards the whole world.

It was at that stage that she started to drink seriously in order to dull the pain of losing her baby, and the children's father disappeared for good from all their lives. The trouble with drink is that although it does help to lessen any pain you might be suffering, it can stoke up any anger that might be simmering below the surface, and Lesley had a cauldron full of that waiting to come to the boil. It also soaks up any spare money there might be in the family, increasing the very hardships that she was trying to escape from.

If there was one thing Lesley was determined not to do, it was be a prisoner in her own home and she became an avid pub drinker and partygoer. She was, after all, still a young woman in her early twenties and she craved a bit of fun. Soon after the divorce had come through she went to a party that Marie – an old school friend of hers – was having to celebrate the anniversary of her marriage to a man called Frankie. Lesley was still a vivacious, attractive young woman and that night she was up for a good time. During the party she met my dad, William, a friend of Marie's and Frankie's, and he appeared to be unattached and interested in her. What she didn't know at the time was that Marie and William were in love but couldn't do anything about it because neither of them wanted to betray Frankie, who William looked on as his best friend.

Believing she was just enjoying a good night out, Lesley was actually stumbling blindly into a love triangle that was already on the brink of exploding.

William was by all accounts a bit of a charmer who could light up a room just by walking into it. He could have had his pick of the women there that night but it was Marie he was in love with and he was beginning to harbour thoughts of trying to coax her away from his mate, Frankie. The first thing he had to do, of course, was ensure that she was as keen to be with him as he was to be with her.

Feeling left out as he watched them together at their anniversary party, and hoping to make Marie jealous on the night, William decided to seduce Lesley, who had probably had enough drinks to make her look like a promising prospect. Ultimately I guess he was hoping that when Marie experienced a rush of jealousy at seeing him paying attention to her friend, she would realize how much she loved him and would leave Frankie for him. It was the sort of game that could only end in tears, but then a lot of people fail to weigh up the consequences of their actions when they're young and they've had a few drinks at a party. Perhaps the flirtation between William and Lesley started out as a relatively innocent bit of fumbling around on the dance floor but one thing soon led to another and a month or two later she found herself pregnant with me.

I don't think Dad was ever the least bit in love with Mum because his affections were always directed towards Marie, even on the night of my conception, but he was a decent man and once he discovered she was pregnant he decided that marrying her was the honourable thing to do. He was a bit daunted to discover that she already had three kids from her first marriage, something she hadn't mentioned when they met at the party, but Mum came from a Catholic family and he realized it would look doubly bad if he didn't put a ring on her finger. The fact that he was willing to marry Lesley, however, did not change the way William still felt about Marie and his plan to kindle her interest by making her jealous was working. Marie had finally decided to give in to his advances, despite the fact that he was now officially engaged to be married to her friend, and was still her husband's best friend. I wasn't even out of the womb and already my family life was a potential war zone. Whatever was going to happen next it was unlikely that anything was going to go smoothly for any of them.

After that night my dad and Marie allowed their passion for one another to overcome all caution and before long Frankie came home unexpectedly one day and caught his wife and his best friend in bed together. Unable to think of anything to say to the treacherous couple, he turned on his heel and walked out of the bedroom without so much as a word. Dad, mortified at what he had done, hurriedly pulled on his trousers and ran after him, but it was too late to save the friendship. The two men started arguing and got into a fight in the street, and when Frankie did eventually come home he took the rest of his anger out on Marie. In that day of betrayal and violence their marriage was destroyed and Dad, furious that any man had dared to lay his fists on the woman he loved, went looking for Frankie again. Everyone now got to hear what was going on, including Lesley. There was no going back; she had a baby on the way and a husband who was having an affair with her best friend. She was publicly humiliated and very, very angry about it.

By the time I was born in 1973 Frankie had disappeared off the scene and Dad was skipping back and forth between Lesley, the mother of his adored first child, and Marie, the love of his life. It was as though I had been born into a powder keg and I was going to be the spark that would ignite the whole thing once and for all. If I had never been conceived I'm sure Dad would never have married Mum and he and Marie would have stayed together from then on and lived a very happy life together. But I was there, and that changed everything.

Chapter Two

A Bitter Battleground

The garage where Dad worked was just a small back-street one, a couple of bays with ramps for the cars to be raised up on when the mechanics needed to get underneath, and some grubby offices and a customers' waiting room to the side, with all the walls smudged in oily handprints. I loved the noise and smell of the place when they were all busy working. If cars didn't need to go on the ramp Dad would sometimes work on them outside on the grass verge beside the road, where Graeme kept a few old bangers polished and lined up for sale at bargain prices. Dad liked being out in the fresh air as he worked and I preferred it too – just him and me and the cars, and the passing world for me to watch.

I always asked him if I could have an oily face like his and I'd squeal with delight when he would rub his fingers over a dirty car engine and then smudge my nose and cheeks as though he was anointing me into some secret Masonic club for car mechanics. If he was working underneath a car he would put me inside his Capri, which would be parked across the forecourt, telling me to stay there and play till he had finished, but if he was working on top of an engine he would pull a high stool up for me beside him and let me fiddle around under the bonnet just like him. Often I was more of a hindrance than a help but he would never get cross when I messed things up, always joking and making me laugh.

I imagine that one of the reasons he liked going to work was because it took him away from the pressures of his private life. No man trying to please two women is likely to be having an easy time of it from either of them, however charming he might be. It was a situation totally of his own making, of course, but that wouldn't have made it any easier to deal with on a day-to-day basis. The easygoing banter of his workmates must have seemed like a rest cure compared to what was going on in his personal life.

Actually, nothing would ever have made Mum an easy person to deal with by then. If she had been angry with life after the loss of her fourth baby and the collapse of her first marriage, she was even angrier when she discovered she now had a husband who was blatantly sleeping with her best friend and making it obvious that he preferred her company. I don't think Dad was making any secret of how he felt about Marie, which must have been hard for Mum to handle, but at the same time I doubt if Mum was making much of an effort to win him back with charm, knowing what her temper was like. It's always hard to know exactly what goes on in other people's relationships and I was certainly too young to understand anything of the emotional whirlwind swirling around me in those first five years of my life. All I knew was that Dad was my protector, whereas Mum was quite likely to give me a beating for no apparent reason if he wasn't looking after me. Maybe my older brothers had undergone exactly the same levels of discipline when they were small, but Dad hadn't been around to protect them. They weren't really his problem. His main concern became keeping me safe from her anger and he did that by having me with him at every possible moment.

Because we were always together and because he made no secret of how much he loved me, Mum began to view me as an extension of him. She saw me as part of the conspiracy against her, part of a team with Dad and Marie, part of her humiliation. Knowing that I was the most precious thing in the world to Dad, she would use me against him whenever she had an opportunity. On one occasion, when I was still a small baby, I'm told she dangled me by the leg from an upstairs window. My father had just stormed out of the house after a row and she shouted at him down in the street below: 'Do you want the little bastard then?'

My father panicked at the sight of me dangling fifteen feet above the hard pavement and ran back. Kicking the front door in he raced upstairs to rescue me, probably aware that she was more than capable of actually dropping me on my head at a moment like that. By the time he burst into the room she had pulled me back to safety, having achieved exactly the reaction she'd wanted. Apparently there was a big fight, in which she ended up with a thick lip and he got two black eyes. He says he'd never raised his hand to a woman before that day but she pushed him too far after risking my life like that. Dad left the house clutching me tightly and vowing to himself that he would never trust her alone with me again.

Mum then called the police to tell them that Dad had abducted me and that she needed their help to get me back. She could be very plausible when talking to people in authority and with her bruised face she wouldn't have had any trouble convincing them that she was the injured party, that she was a good and dutiful mother who had her child's best interests at heart, while Dad was a violent philanderer who should never be trusted to look after a baby. By hitting her and grabbing me he had inadvertently played into her hands, making her look like the innocent victim of a brutal man. The police got involved and instructed him to give me back, which meant he had to come back too if he wasn't going to risk leaving me alone with her. It must have been an agonizing choice for him and it must have made him resent Mum all the more for forcing him into a corner.

As far as Mum was concerned, of course, her plan of using me to blackmail Dad into giving up Marie and staying with her had temporarily paid off. Not wanting to lose his son, knowing that I would need him there to protect me from her anger, he was forced to come home. She had gambled on him being more frightened of losing me than of losing Marie and the gamble had paid off, although not for long. He must have felt as though he was being torn in half, unable to give either of us up but constantly frightened of what Mum might do next. Even though he was back living in the house he was always nervous about leaving me alone in a room with her and he would take me everywhere with him, especially to work and also to Marie's house when he could no longer resist the temptation to be with her.

It wasn't long before Mum realized that her plan wasn't working and that his feelings for Marie were too strong for him to be able to stay away from her, as long as he felt that I was safe. It must have been galling for Mum to know that he preferred to be with Marie and she saw me as an accomplice in his behaviour, another enemy, even though I was far too young to understand what was going on between the grown-ups in my life.

Despite the explosive nature of their relationship, or maybe because of it, Mum and Dad still managed to get it together enough during their periods of reconciliation for her to fall pregnant by him twice more, giving birth to a girl called Ellie, born eighteen months after me, and then a boy called Thomas, who was almost three years younger than me. I suppose there must have been some positive passion in their relationship as well as all that anger for them to continue creating a family in the midst of their battles.

From the moment she was born, my sister Ellie was Mum's favourite, her little angel, and she never seemed to want to hurt her in the way she did me. Thomas was treated badly, but she didn't hate him with the same depth of loathing that she harboured for me. With a strange kind of warped logic, she blamed me for Dad's misdemeanours but not the other two. Maybe it was because I was so clearly his favourite. Maybe it was because I looked so much like him.

People who knew our family at that time tell me that Dad never became as obsessed about the other two as he was with me. Maybe he didn't think they were in the same danger from Mum as I was. Maybe he could sense that my mother harboured a dislike for me that went far beyond anything rational. Perhaps he deliberately kept his other two children at arm's length in the hope that she would bond with them better if she didn't associate them with him and Marie. Or maybe he just liked having me around because I was that little bit older and adored him so completely. Once he had a boy to be his constant companion, perhaps he didn't feel that he needed any more. I've got no idea what he was thinking or feeling during those early years of my life. I just know he was my hero, my pal and my protector.

Soon after Thomas was born, Mum and Dad decided to try to patch everything up once and for all. Dad reluctantly parted from Marie and went back home to attempt to be a father to all six of us (including three step-kids), but he still made sure I was always under his watchful eye. Terrified of being hit I would cling tighter to him and the closer I stuck to him the more annoyed Mum became with me. Her hatred of me seemed to grow deeper every day. The attempt at reconciliation soon floundered and by the time I was four Dad and I were more or less living full time with Marie. Mum's desperate attempts to hold onto her second marriage had failed and she was finally losing him. He was setting a divorce in motion and all she could do was rage against us to anyone who would listen. I dare say she got a fair bit of sympathy as she was the deserted party, but anyone who knew what she was like in the privacy of her own home would never have been surprised that Dad had chosen Marie over her.

In his determination to keep me out of her grasp Dad went to the courts to say that Mum was an unfit mother to me and that I would be in danger if he left me with her. There were hearings and discussions with the welfare services and his sister Melissa has since told me that she began to believe that Dad was becoming overly protective and obsessive about me. No one in the outside world could know what Mum was really like towards me.

Dad's relationship with Mum had reached such a low point at one stage that he became convinced Thomas wasn't his child. I don't think he was right, but someone must have told him something about seeing Mum messing about with another man that had made him suspicious and once those suspicions took a hold he didn't seem to be able to shake them off. Maybe subconsciously he wanted Mum to have betrayed him so he wouldn't feel so bad about his affair with Marie. Or maybe he thought Thomas would be safer from Mum's campaign of revenge if it turned out that he had been fathered by another man.

Marie must have been desperately in love with Dad to have put up with so much and to have continued to take him back even after he had got Mum pregnant twice more. When he went back to Marie for the final time Dad promised her he was going to divorce Mum on the grounds of her adultery, although I don't know how he thought he was going to be able to prove it. Marie told me with great excitement that she and Dad were going to get married one day soon and we would be a happy family together. I was delighted about this and couldn't wait until it was all sorted, but they must have been painful, turbulent times for all the adults involved.

Marie then fell pregnant as well, adding yet another layer of anger and bitterness to the store that Mum was building up inside her head. This final insult tipped her over the edge and she actually went looking for Marie with physical revenge on her mind, like some bizarre sort of Wild West gunslinger. When she found her she beat her up badly, pouring all her anger and resentment into her punches. It would be impossible to overstate just how strong my mother was when she lost her temper; she was still slim at this stage but she was such a tall woman that no one was a match for her when she was angry. To us who were on the receiving end it was almost as though she was possessed by demons.

The beating made Marie all the more nervous and anxious to stay out of her way and not to annoy Mum any more than she had to. Occasionally when I was with Marie I would slip up and call her 'Mum', because that is what she seemed like to me – far more maternal than the screaming, battering woman I had been born to. She would quickly correct me and tell me to call her 'Auntie Marie', terrified that if Mum found out what I was doing that she would go completely mad, seeing it as yet more evidence that Marie was trying to steal her child as well as her husband. Mum might not have wanted anything to do with me herself, but she certainly wouldn't have wanted Marie to have the satisfaction of taking me away from her.

While they waited for the divorce to grind its way through the system Marie changed her surname to Peters so that we would seem more like a family unit. She even took to wearing a wedding ring because in those days around our way there was still a stigma attached to single mothers in many people's eyes.

But the shadow of Mum and her wild, violent temper was always hanging over Dad and Marie, making them both nervous in different ways, always looking over their shoulders, expecting her to pounce at any moment shouting abuse and throwing punches. My younger siblings and I were a link that would always be there, never letting Dad escape completely from this unwise, youthful alliance.

One day he received a call from Mum to tell him that Thomas, who was not yet two, had been taken into hospital covered in burns. By that stage Dad must have accepted that Thomas was his because he rushed straight to the hospital. Thomas had been admitted into an intensive care unit, with burns all the way down one side of his body from his head to his waist.

'There was a pan of boiling water on the stove,' Mum told him when he asked her what had happened. 'He was sitting on the floor and Larry slipped and knocked the pan all over him.'

I doubt if Dad believed her story, however convincingly she told it, but there was little he could do to prove she was lying until later, when my oldest half-brother Wally confessed that what had actually happened was that Thomas wouldn't stop crying and so Mum had thrown him into a bath of scalding water in a fit of temper. Whatever the truth, Thomas was left badly scarred and needed endless skin grafts over the following years. Dad was angry enough when he heard Mum's own version of the story, wanting to know why she wasn't watching over such a small baby more carefully. When he found out Wally's version of events he immediately brought Ellie to live with us at Marie's, while Thomas stayed on in hospital, struggling for his little life. Dad might not have been as close to Thomas or Ellie as he was to me, but he still didn't intend to leave them to the mercy of a woman who was capable of doing such things to a defenceless small child.

Mum, however, wasn't about to allow him to walk off with her precious Ellie and she was constantly coming round to Marie's house, banging furiously on the door, screaming abuse and demanding they give her children back, laying into Dad and Marie with her fists whenever she had a chance, bringing in the welfare workers and arguing her case for being allowed to keep her own children rather than handing them over to her husband's 'whore'. There was no way she was ever going to give in quietly and go away so in the end Dad was forced to compromise and allow Ellie to go back to her since she had never done her any harm. When Thomas was eventually released from hospital, Mum grabbed him and took him home and there was nothing Dad could do about it. But he wasn't going to let me go. For a while it looked as if Mum might be going to settle for that and give up picking fights over me, but not for long.

After the day Mum grabbed me from Aunt Melissa's, dragged me home and burned my hand on the iron, Dad reported the incident to social services and they duly went to interview Mum. Yet again she managed to convince them that it was Dad who was the violent one, not her, and she was able to show them the bruises where he had punched her when they were struggling over me. She could be incredibly convincing when she wanted to be. It was as though she was two different people: the one who faced the outside world with a sweet smile, and then the monster who erupted once we were behind closed doors. She was brilliant at convincing anyone in authority, such as teachers and social workers, that she was a wonderful mother, struggling bravely on with bringing up her children alone. For them she would put on a wonderful act and anyone who knew her better was too frightened to contradict, allowing her to keep up her respectable façade in the eyes of the outside world.

I didn't have any problem about being with Dad all the time, and when I was little his employers were very understanding about having me around the garage, even when I caused trouble – like the time when I let the handbrake off in his Capri while I was locked inside to play. I can clearly remember the horrified look on Dad's face as the car rolled steadily down towards the main road with him desperately trying to hold it back, calling out to me to pull up the locks so he could get in while I was laughing happily at all the attention, jumping up and down with excitement. I must only have been about three at the time, maybe just four.

'Good boy,' Dad kept shouting. 'Open the door! Open the door!'

It wasn't till we were out in the road that I realized the danger and by that time it was too late and the car was travelling too fast for me to be able to get the door open in time. People scattered in every direction at the sound of Dad's shouting and fortunately we managed to get right across the road without hitting any of the passing traffic or pedestrians, the car dragging Dad along with it. We eventually came to a halt against a wall with a hedge on top. The impact sent me flying and my head banged hard against the dashboard. Not wanting to leave me in order to run and get the key, and still unable to persuade me to unlock the door in my dazed state, Dad smashed the window and pulled up the lock himself. When he finally managed to pull me out he hugged me so tightly I could hardly breathe. He was crying from the shock of the whole thing and never even told me off. He probably let me get away with more than he should have, but I certainly wasn't complaining about that.

No one in the garage minded that Dad brought me to work – he had been there so long he was pretty much the boss – but it became harder for them to turn a blind eye when Mum started turning up and causing fights, trying to get me back from him, accusing him of kidnapping me, ranting on about his 'whore'. I'm sure she didn't actually want me, unless it was to get the benefit payments; she just didn't want him and Marie to have something that she believed belonged to her. She had heard about the handbrake incident and tried to use it to prove that Dad was being an irresponsible parent by taking me to work with him. She never missed a trick in their on-going war.

More often than not she would be drunk when she decided to make these visits to the garage, and she would always be spoiling for a physical fight if she could provoke Dad into giving her one. Whenever he saw her lurching in through the doors Dad would shout to the other lads working there, telling them to take me into the office out of harm's way and we would watch the two of them battling it out through the windows. I already knew that I didn't like my own mother. I was scared of her and watching her in action through the grimy glass made me all the more certain I wanted to stay with Dad and Marie.

'Come to Mummy,' she would say, holding her arms out to me as if she expected me to run joyfully into them, but I wouldn't be able to move, rigid with fear at the very sight of her. Even when I knew Dad was there to protect me I would still pee myself with fright when she started shouting at me. She always seemed to be shouting and screaming, attacking everyone and throwing spanners and other tools around. If she managed to get close enough she would scratch at Dad's face and eyes as he struggled to restrain her.

Dad wanted to avoid hitting her himself if he could help it, so he used to call his sister Melissa, who lived nearby, and get her to come and sort Mum out for him. Aunt Melissa loved my dad, just as everyone did, and would do anything to protect her little brother. She would come charging down the street and the two women would have the most colossal fights outside on the garage forecourt, pulling one another around by the hair, slapping and kicking with all their strength. Aunt Melissa would always win so after a while Mum started to run away as soon as she saw her coming, diving into a waiting car that one of her drinking buddies from the pub would have brought her over in, the driver revving away like a bank robber on the run. I think Mum enjoyed the drama of it as much as anything else.

The harassment was continuous, with Mum endlessly ringing the house and the garage as well as turning up looking for fights. She used to scratch the paintwork of Dad's car and smash Marie's windows with bricks, trying everything she could think of in her campaign of hate and revenge. Eventually it became too much and Graeme, the garage owner, had to tell Dad that the constant scenes with Mum had to stop because they were starting to upset customers and interrupt business. He couldn't allow them to go on if it was making customers too nervous to come in. He called one evening and asked Dad to meet him the next day for a chat about what they should do. That night Marie and Dad discussed the situation.

'It's not good for Joe to have to keep witnessing these scenes,' she said. 'You need to leave him at home with me. He's five years old and he'll be starting school soon enough – I can just keep an eye on him till then.'

'No, no,' Dad was adamant. 'Lesley'll be round here to get him if I do that. He likes coming down the garage anyway.'

It was brave of Marie to offer to look after me because she was as scared of Mum's violence as everyone else was, apart from Aunt Melissa. Mum was a tough woman, who was able and willing to hit hard. She was capable of knocking grown men out with a single punch, let alone a petite woman like Marie. Marie and Dad talked about it endlessly that night and eventually he agreed that he should at least leave me at home with her the next day while he went in to discuss with Graeme what they were going to do about the situation.

So I stayed with Marie the next morning and Dad came back at lunchtime to get his tools. He always had his own special set of tools that he guarded with his life and wouldn't let anyone else touch, not even his mates at the garage.

'I've told Graeme I'll get a court order to keep her away from the garage,' he said. 'But he thinks that if Joe doesn't come to the garage for a bit that will mean she'll stay away too.'

I was standing listening to them as he collected up his tools and went towards the door. He glanced back at me.

'Do you want to come to work with your dad?' he asked with a wink.

'No,' Marie interrupted. 'What would Graeme say if he found out?'

'Graeme's not there this afternoon,' he wheedled. 'He's all right. Just one more time. It won't hurt him.'

'I'm not happy about this, William,' Marie protested. 'You don't want to risk losing your job.'

'It'll never come to that,' Dad insisted, so Marie gave in and let me go.

That was an afternoon I'll never forget as long as I live, the afternoon my life changed for ever. I can remember every single detail of every little thing that happened that day, because the details are etched on my brain and thirty years on I still relive them in my nightmares. As I slipped my hand inside Dad's big fingers and walked out to the car that lunchtime, I had no idea that life as I knew it was about to come to a brutal end.

Chapter Three

Inferno

It was a cold, windy day in February. Dad and I had just driven up to the garage and parked on the grass verge when one of the other mechanics, a good friend of Dad's called Derek, waved him over to a car that was up on one of the ramps.

'Can you smell petrol, William?' Derek asked. 'I've looked all over but I can't find where it's coming from.'

'You get back in the car,' Dad said to me. 'This'll only take a minute.'

I would rather have helped him with his job, but I didn't bother to ask because I knew he would say no, and I knew he would come back for me as soon as he had sorted out the problem. He'd explained to me lots of times how car engines were dangerous things and he couldn't risk having me messing around with them unless he was able to watch me all the time. There weren't many things Dad insisted on when he was with me, but that was one of them.

He turned the key in the lock of the Ford Capri and I watched through the windscreen as he went over with Derek to examine the damaged engine. I didn't mind waiting. I loved being at the garage with Dad, even though he had told me this might be the last time we could do it for a while because of all the trouble Mum had been causing for him.

I sat behind the steering wheel in his driving seat and rattled the gear stick around, imitating the movements I'd seen him make when he was driving. I idolized him and wanted to be like him in every way possible. I wasn't worried about the locked car doors because I knew perfectly well how to open them if I wanted to. Dad had explained it to me very carefully after that time I let the handbrake off. But I wouldn't have disobeyed him because I respected him completely. If he said I was to stay there then that was what I would do. He had never had to raise his hand to me in my whole life because I never gave him cause to. I would have followed him to the ends of the earth and never questioned a single thing he told me to do.

Through the windscreen I watched Dad lying down on the greasy garage floor in his overalls like I'd seen him do a hundred times before and sliding under the car to see if he could spot where the petrol was leaking from.

It was just another normal day at work for all of them. I heard the phone in the office ringing, the giant bell in the workshop going off like a fire alarm to make sure that it could always be heard above the revving of engines and the clanking of tools. Derek went into the office to answer it.

'Dad,' I shouted out through the crack in the window, knowing exactly what his answer would be even before I asked the question, 'can I come under the car with you?'

'No,' he shouted back, as I knew he would. 'You stay there. I won't be a minute.'

As I went back to playing with the gear stick and steering wheel I saw a customer coming out of the waiting room with a cigarette in the corner of his mouth. He had the collar of his jacket turned up against the cold. I didn't really know what petrol was; it had always looked just like water to me whenever I'd seen it – water with a funny smell. So I didn't think anything of it as I watched the man casually flick his fag end towards the main door of the garage, where the wind picked it up and bounced it back across the floor, making the still-burning tip glow fiercely.

One minute there was nothing happening, everything continuing as normal, and the next there were huge orange-red flames roaring up around the car that Dad was lying under. I could see his silhouette in the middle of the inferno wriggling its way out and rising through the flames and I started to scream for him, my little boy's voice trapped inside the car just yards away while the fire roared around him outside.

'Dad! Dad!'

An explosion lifted the car he had been under into the air and flipped it onto its side, like a special effect from some action film or television programme, making the Ford Capri rock from the blast and knocking me over onto the seat. Dad had managed to get to his feet but his whole body was on fire as he ran around the garage, screaming with a mixture of pain and terror, unable to escape the flames that clung to him, his movement making them burn fiercer. The other men, including Derek, all came running out of the office and stared in horror. It was as though time had frozen as they all stood there in shock, watching Dad. Every second seemed like an hour as the flames grew more ferocious, fanned by the wind, which returned through the doors once the blast had died away and took a firmer hold on their victim. As I struggled with the locks of the Capri door, desperate to get to him, all I could see was him running around and his screams filled my ears. I thought no one was doing anything to help him but I found out later that Derek had been struggling with a fire extinguisher, unable to get it to work.

A neighbour from across the road, who had heard the explosion, came running in through the entrance, grabbed Dad and threw him onto the floor, trying to beat the flames out. I finally managed to get out of the Capri and ran across to where Dad was lying. By the time I got there the flames were out and everything was black and charred. His whole body was shaking and convulsing and going into shock. Derek grabbed me and covered my eyes with his hand before I could see Dad's incinerated face close up. I remember the smell, though – a sickly smell of burned flesh and choking smoke. I could hear the sound of sirens coming closer and people running around as I struggled to get free, kicking and biting, frantic to get to my dad. Derek kept holding me tight so that I didn't get in the way of the rescuers, protecting me from the full impact of the sight.

The ambulance men lifted Dad onto a stretcher and loaded him into the back of the ambulance.

'Let me come with you. Dad, tell them to let me come!' I cried, tears streaming down my face, but the ambulance men said no, they couldn't have a child on board.

Derek phoned my Aunt Melissa and she rushed over within a few minutes. She tried to comfort me as best she could but she was too worried about her brother to think clearly about anything. To me at that moment it felt like the whole world had ended in that explosion of horror. I was just five years old. I wanted my dad back.

Chapter Four

'Turn Him Off!'

The ambulance carried Dad off at full speed, all sirens blaring. I watched it go and then Aunt Melissa led me up the road to her house and phoned Marie to let her know what had happened. When Marie arrived, I remember lots of hushed whispers and glances that I wasn't meant to see. Melissa's husband Amani, a big Nigerian guy, kept staring at me and I remember I felt uncomfortable and didn't want him there.

'When can I go to the hospital to see my dad?' I kept asking. I knew his burns must be hurting a lot. I could remember clearly how much it had hurt when Mum had pressed my hand against the flat of the iron, so I thought I could imagine what agonies my dad must be going through after being completely engulfed in flames and I wanted to go and try to comfort him. I couldn't get the image of him running around the garage on fire out of my head. I didn't like being parted from him when I was so worried about what was going on. I felt exposed and vulnerable. All the bad things that had ever happened to me had always happened when he wasn't there to protect me and I didn't know how long it would be before he was able to come out of hospital and be there for me again. I kept asking the adults questions but none of them had any answers for me. Everyone was crying.

Marie took me home a few hours later. Being with her always felt more like being at home than when I was in the house where my mother lived. I was in a state of complete shock, unable to take in what I had witnessed and the pictures that kept going round and round in my head, having no idea what it was all going to mean to me. It didn't occur to me for a moment that my dad might actually die; I didn't know what death was at that age. I was worried for him and horrified to have heard him screaming so terribly, but I assumed the doctors would make him better and he would be back to look after me soon with nothing more than a few scars to remind us of that terrible day – just as they had made Thomas and me better when we had been burned.

Marie tried to talk to me and prepare me for what might happen. 'Sometimes, when people are very badly hurt,' she said, 'they die and they go to Heaven to be with God. It's a beautiful place, and they can look down on everyone they love and watch out for them from up there.'

I listened, but as if she was telling me a fairy story. I didn't for one moment think that she was saying this might happen to my dad. I was just waiting until I could see him again, convinced that he would make everything all right once the doctors had fixed his burns.

I wasn't allowed to go in to visit him until three days later. I don't know if the hospital had been permitting visitors before that, but Marie must have known Mum would be there and perhaps she didn't want to take me in and risk her snatching me away. Or maybe she had thought it would be too traumatic for me to see Dad in that state but I just nagged until she gave in. She must have been as shocked by the accident as I was, even though she was a grown-up. All her instincts must have been to run to be by the bedside of the man she loved, but I suppose she was nervous about Mum starting a fight on the ward. By the time she did take me in to see him they knew that he was going to die and she must have decided I should be given a chance to say goodbye. He was already brain dead but I had no idea about that as I walked in holding tightly to her hand.

I clung to Marie as we passed through the seemingly endless corridors of the hospital, constantly on the watch for Mum, expecting her to jump out round every corner we turned. When we finally reached the intensive care ward it was all quiet, each bed surrounded by equipment that buzzed and blinked as it supported the lives of the patients it was attached to. We stopped beside a bed and I tried to work out what I was looking at. The bandaged figure lying unconscious on the mattress with tubes coming in and out of him didn't look like my dad. At first I didn't believe it was him. I thought they'd made a mistake and brought me to the wrong bed.

'Where's Dad?' I asked Marie. 'What have they done with him?'

'This is your dad, Joe,' Marie said gently and I could see there were tears glinting in her eyes.

It must have been just as upsetting for her to see him like that as it was for me but she had to stay brave and not break down in front of me. A nurse was standing by the head of the bed checking something on a monitor, and she gave me a sympathetic look.

I turned again to the bandaged figure on the bed. Parts of him were covered in clear bags of fluid, which seemed to me at the time to be dripping and seeping with blood and raw flesh but it was probably just that I could see through them to the terrible burns underneath. The machines made a heavy sighing sound, and Dad's chest was moving up and down but his face was so heavily bandaged that I couldn't see his eyes or his mouth.

'Dad?' I said tentatively, but the word came out funny, as if it was catching in my throat.

'He can't talk,' Marie explained, stroking my hair.

I started to back away from the bed, overcome with horror at the sight before my eyes. Marie must have realized that she had made a mistake in giving in to my nagging and bringing me to the hospital, but it was too late by then. Suddenly Mum appeared on the other side of the bed, making me jump and shiver with fright, certain she was going to launch herself at us as she always did on her visits to the garage. But she was behaving differently this time, playing the traumatized young wife for the benefit of the watching nurse. It didn't last long. Her grief changed to anger as soon as we were left alone round the bed. I could see from her furious face that she certainly wasn't pleased to see Marie.

'What the fuck are you doing here?' she snarled as soon as the nurse was out of earshot. 'He's my fucking husband, not yours.'

There was nothing Marie could say in her defence. Because they were still officially married Mum was Dad's next of kin and the nurses and doctors had to deal with her when it came to talking about Dad's condition and asking for decisions. It didn't make any difference to them that he had been about to divorce her. Marie was cut out completely from all the medical information and from all the arrangements, which obviously pleased Mum. As long as Dad was unconscious she had complete power over all of us.

Although I didn't realize it at the time, Dad was only alive because of the life support machine.

'Anyway, the doctors have told me there's no way he's going to pull through,' Mum said. 'They think it's time to turn the machine off, but the final decision is up to me.'

Marie gave a gasp and put her hand to her mouth. 'No, Lesley. Please don't. Don't give up hope. There might still be a chance.'

I clung to Marie's arm, trying to make sense of what they were saying, but I knew from the look on Mum's face that she had made up her mind about something. Something important.

'He was no good as a husband before and he's certainly no good to me now.' Mum was revelling in her ability to make such a life and death decision about the man who she believed had betrayed her so badly, enjoying the ultimate revenge, no longer bothering to keep up any pretence at being the grieving widow.

'He was divorcing you,' Marie protested. 'He was living with me. I'm his next of kin, not you. I should make the decision.'

'I'm his legal wife,' Mum screamed, making heads turn and bringing the nurses running to calm things down. 'You're just his whore!'

Marie tried to explain the situation to the nurses and one of them ran off to find a doctor, but it was no good.

If Dad had been able to speak he would have said that he wanted Marie to handle everything and Mum to be nowhere near the place, but there was no way he was ever going to speak again. Marie realized there was nothing she could do, that Mum had the law on her side, but still she tried to plead with the staff.

'It's my decision,' Mum insisted to the doctor, 'and I say turn him off!'

Overcome with grief Marie kept fighting back even though she probably knew she didn't have a chance of changing Mum's mind, begging her to think again, but Mum was becoming angrier and angrier that Marie was daring to challenge her decision. The argument escalated into more and more noise until hospital security had to be called to stop them resorting to blows and Marie was told she would have to leave the premises.

'You can leave him here with me,' Mum said, gesturing towards me. I shrank as far behind Marie as I could.

'No way. He's staying with me,' Marie insisted, gripping my hand tightly. 'It's what William would have wanted.'

She knew that Dad would never have wanted me to go back there and she was already frightened of what Mum would do once she got me alone. Knowing she had the law on her side, Mum asked the hospital staff to call the police. There was no way she was going to allow Marie to keep something that was hers, even though she didn't really want me herself. Marie stood firm and we all waited as the staff circled nervously around us.

When the police arrived they separated the two women off into different rooms and interviewed Marie first. I clung to her as she tried to explain how Dad had been allowed to have custody of me because of the way Mum had treated me in the past, and how his one wish was always that Mum shouldn't be allowed to get her hands on me. But there was nothing she could say that could make any difference to the facts of the situation; I legally belonged to Mum and if she said I was to go back to her then I was going to have to go. The police probably couldn't see what the problem was, knowing that Mum was already bringing up five other children. I listened without fully understanding what was being said, until a policewoman knelt down beside me.

'You have to go with your mummy now,' she said, and I started screaming 'No! Don't make me!'

There was nothing Marie could do any more. We went out into the corridor where Mum was still gloating.

'They've turned him off now. There's nothing more to hang around for. Come on, Joe.'

Marie burst into tears as Mum dragged me, sobbing, towards the exit. Just a few days earlier Marie had imagined she was going to spend the rest of her life with Dad, bringing me up as if I was her own son. Now she was a single mother and my baby half-brother, born just a couple of months before the accident, was all she had left to remember my father by.

As we walked home, Mum made sure I knew what had happened. 'Your dad's dead now. He ain't coming back. He's fucking dead,' she told me.

'Has he gone to Heaven?' I asked through my tears.

'No, he's gone to hell where all the nasty people go! God said he was no good and so now his body is going to be burned to ashes. It was God who threw that cigarette into the petrol but he didn't do a good enough job, did he? So now his body is going to be taken to an oven and burned until it has crumbled to pieces.'

As she talked I remembered watching the burning cigarette end bouncing back into the garage, carried by that fateful wind. Was that the hand of God I had witnessed at work there? Who else would have been able to control the wind like that? Her sneering words had a horrible kind of logic to them and I was left with a picture of my dad burning in hell for all eternity, just as I'd seen him do when he ran around the garage.

I was crying so hard I could hardly breathe.

'Don't think you're anything special,' she told me, squeezing my hand viciously, 'just because you were your dad's favourite, and just because you saw him going up in fucking flames. You're not special at all. You're nothing, and I'm going to prove it to you. Just you fuck-ing wait.'

Chapter Five

Smelly Woof

From the moment we walked in the door of Mum's big end-of-terrace Victorian council house, I was under no illusions at all about my place in the family pecking order. Far from being special, I was relegated to bottom of the heap. Larry and Barry appeared in the hall, and Larry's first words were 'I see the little bastard's back,' before he kicked me and Barry punched me on the arm.

Mum called Wally downstairs and explained to the three of them that I had been spoiled rotten by my dad and needed to learn my place in the family as the lowest of the low. Having been Dad's favourite I was seen as being part of his betrayal of her, and it wasn't hard for her to persuade the others that I was a spoiled brat who thought he was better than them.

Whereas Wally, my eldest brother, now aged seventeen, was inclined to be sympathetic to me because I was such a small child who had been through such a terrible trauma, Larry and Barry, aged fifteen and fourteen respectively, were more than happy to be given permission to indulge the vicious streaks that ran through their natures and to treat me as badly as possible. They were like bloodthirsty soldiers who had been given permission by their commanding officer to rape and pillage an enemy they had been brainwashed into believing was subhuman. Mum made it clear that showing me sympathy was not allowed. If Wally wasn't going to join in my persecution he could expect to be on the receiving end of beatings himself. It all seemed very simple to her; if you weren't on her team then you were obviously with the enemy.

Ellie and Thomas (then aged four and three) were still too little to play any part in my humiliation. I guess to their wide, innocent eyes it all seemed like normal family life because they had never known any different. In fact I was the only one who had lived with anyone else, the only one who realized that life didn't have to be this terrifying and this painful all the time.

'He'll sleep on the floor in your room,' Mum told Larry and Barry. 'He's not good enough for a room of his own. Take him up there and get him out of my sight.'

They were happy to oblige, kicking and punching me all the way up the stairs before pushing me into their bedroom.

The house was four storeys high, as tall as a tower to a small, frightened boy. It had a railway line running directly beside it, the trains making the sturdy walls tremble every time they rattled past. I crouched by the window, shaking, and gradually my fear was turning to anger. The only thing I wanted was to see my dad again and the frustration at not being able to do that was building inside my head like a volcano waiting to erupt. When Larry and Barry came to fetch me for dinner, I lashed out at them, biting, kicking and punching, earning myself a clout round the ear and, I suppose, fulfilling Mum's description of me as a spoiled brat.

The family dining table was made of glass, with steel legs attached to the underneath by what looked like giant suckers. I went to sit down at it that first evening and Mum sneered, 'No, you're not good enough to sit with us. Get down on the floor, under the table, and we'll feed you scraps, like a dog.'

Larry and Barry wrestled me to the floor, and thus began a new pattern in which this was how all my meals were fed to me. As I crouched under the table, they would kick out at me and drop scraps on the floor, grinding them into the tiles with the heels of their shoes and then ordering me to lick them up with my tongue. They would actually make me jump up and down and beg for my food like a dog.

I might have fought back if it was just my brothers but with Mum I already knew I had to be more careful how I behaved because of the fearsomeness of her violence and the willingness with which she would dispense it. After a few more beatings for looking at her the wrong way, or answering her back, the message got home to me once and for all and I realized I was not going to get any preferential treatment just because I had lost my father — quite the opposite in fact. I quickly learned not to do anything to antagonize her any more than I did simply by being there. My very existence was a constant reminder of Dad and his treachery, but even doing nothing wasn't going to save me from what was to come. To the outside world she seemed like a tragic grieving widow coping with a traumatized child; to those of us who lived with her she was a vindictive, vengeful, violent force of nature.

'You're nothing special,' she kept reminding me, over and over again. 'Don't you fucking forget it.'

The day after Mum brought me back to her house, I overheard a conversation on the phone between her and Marie. My ears pricked up when I heard her name, hoping that she was going to come and fetch me back to hers, but it wasn't to be.

'I tell you what,' Mum said to her, unable to resist another round of gloating. 'You can fucking have him now. He's no use to anyone any more, is he? I'll let you take care of the funeral.'

I didn't understand what they were talking about but I found out later from Wally that Mum was refusing to pay for a funeral and insisting that Marie covered it. Marie had her own little market stall at the time selling perfumes and cosmetics so Mum knew she had a bit of money and she knew she wouldn't want to refuse to do something for Dad. But even at that stage Mum still wasn't going to let go of her powers as the legal wife that easily. Although Dad had always believed in having a burial, she insisted that his body be cremated.

'She may be paying,' she told the poor embarrassed funeral directors, 'but I'm his wife so I get to say what happens, and I say he goes to the crematorium.'

Marie put up a bit of a fight. 'But William always believed in burial,' she protested. 'You know that.'

'If you don't agree to the cremation,' Mum replied, 'I'll pay for the fucking funeral myself and I won't be letting you through the fucking doors.'

Even though she knew Mum didn't have the money, Marie was aware that it wasn't an idle threat. If she wanted to say her last goodbyes to Dad she had no choice but to do as Mum wanted.

After Wally had explained to me what a funeral was, I begged Mum to let me come along to Dad's, but there was no chance of that. She was playing the role of grieving widow and I suppose it would have spoiled the act if I had run over to cling to Marie during the ceremony rather than her.

'You all right, Bro?' Wally asked me now and then, giving me a comforting cuddle if no one else was watching, and I would nod gratefully, even though I wasn't all right at all. I felt that he understood a bit of what I was going through and I wished it was just him and me living there with the little ones.

Being only five years old I'd had no concept of death until I was told that Dad had gone. Marie had talked about heaven, but Mum said he'd gone to hell. I'd never even had to think about it before. So my way of finding out about it was by discovering that the one person in the world I loved above all others had gone for good; that I was never going to see him again, or talk to him, or ask him any questions or take shelter behind his long legs. It felt as though I had been hit with a sledgehammer, the weight of my misery crushing me into the ground.

Occasionally Wally would try to put things right for me in a hushed whisper when he was sure Mum was out of the house. 'Don't listen to Mummy,' he would say under his breath, 'she's wrong. Your dad has gone to heaven, not hell.' I wanted to believe him, but I was afraid he was just being kind and that it was Mum who was telling the truth. She was the grown up after all, I reasoned, and she was my mother; why would she lie to me about something so important? Nothing made any sense any more.

Mum kept the house in immaculate condition, obsessively cleaning and tidying all day long. It was a show home although hardly anyone other than her and her children was ever allowed to set foot through the door. None of us dared to make a mess because it could result in her exploding with fury. Apart from drinking and beating her children about, housework was all Mum ever did. It was as though she was trying to control every object and every speck of dirt in her little kingdom. Each morning she would be up at half past five sweeping round the paths outside the house and vacuuming every dustless room. The towels in the bathroom were lined up in perfect sequence and even the bar of soap by the bath would be positioned at exactly the correct angle. No one was allowed to sit on a chair or settee in case they dented the cushions; we all had to sit on the floor. Before she went to bed at night she would lay out all the breakfast bowls for the morning, every setting lined up and every portion of cereal measured out and ready. The immaculate state of the house added to the image of her as the admirable mother in the eyes of any visiting authorities. If she was looking after her home this well, they must have reasoned, she must be caring for her children with equal passion and dedication.

As my overwhelming grief and anger began to erupt as tantrums, in which I threw cups and plates across the room, and lashed out, kicking and biting my brothers, Mum stepped in quickly. Having a disturbed five-year-old smashing the place up in temper was far more than she was ever going to be willing to tolerate. I had to be brought under control instantly and completely, so that I would obey her as readily and blindly as the others did. She didn't intend to teach me how to behave better with love and encouragement, which is how most mothers would have approached the problem; she intended to break my spirit in every way possible. She couldn't be bothered to try to find out what was troubling me and work towards helping me come to terms with the shock that had traumatized every atom of my body.

To achieve instant results she needed first to isolate me from the rest of the world, from anyone who might disagree with her methods and might show some sympathy for me rather than for her. In the early days some of Dad's family came round hoping to visit me and see how I was getting on, but Mum wouldn't allow any of them through the door or anywhere near me. She wanted to keep prying eyes away from what was really happening inside her home, inside the kingdom that she ruled with a rod of iron. If they came knocking she would order them off her property with a stream of threats and obscenities.

'Fuck off out of it,' she screamed into their faces, 'or I'm calling the police. Go on, fuck off out of it!'

She'd always hated them all, particularly Aunt Melissa, and now Dad was gone she felt she didn't have to put up with any of them sticking their noses into her business any more, telling her how to bring up her children. I was her son and as far as she was concerned it was nothing to do with them how I was getting on. I was more than just her son; I was her sole property now that Dad had gone, to do with as she pleased.

Within a few days of me arriving, I was told that I was only ever allowed to wear my underpants because I didn't 'deserve' to have any clothes. If I refused to obey any of her orders I would be violently punished, so I quickly learned always to do as she told me.

I was only allowed to use the bathroom when she said I could so I soon became unkempt and dirty, in contrast to the immaculate cleanliness of the rest of the house. Then because I was so dirty I wasn't allowed to use any of Mum's crockery in case I spread my germs and diseases to the others.

'You've inherited the "dirty disease" from your filthy fucking father,' Mum told me. 'I don't want you infecting the rest of us.'

When you're little you believe whatever your mother tells you, so I assumed it must all be true, that I must be inferior to the others in some way. The fact that I was the family dog became a standing joke and later they bought me a metal dog's bowl for my Christmas present, laughing happily at their own wit as they gave it to me. It was as though I was there to entertain them. They were constantly thinking up new ways to amuse themselves, like offering me my meal in the bowl and then throwing the food at me anyway, or spitting on it before making me eat it up, saliva and all. They called me 'Smelly Woof' when they were pretending I was their pet, and I knew I did smell, mostly of my own wee, which would escape me involuntarily when fear overcame me and I lost control of my bladder. If I had been allowed a bath occasionally maybe I wouldn't have stunk the house up and made them all so disgusted with me.

As the days went past a mixture of shock, fear and grief was taking control of my head and sometimes it wouldn't let the words come out of my mouth. There were so many things I wanted to say but when I tried to talk the muscles in my throat would seem to freeze, refusing to obey me, making me stammer and stutter as I attempted to force the words out. It felt as though someone was trying to strangle me into silence. All I could think about was my dad. I was constantly seeing the pictures of him burning and Mum's words going round and round in my head. I tried to say, 'I want to see my dad', even though I knew the words would earn me another beating, but as I struggled to find them my tongue would stumble. Wally was the first to notice that I was stuttering.

'I'm worried about Joe,' he said to Mum.

'What's fucking wrong with him now?' she wanted to know.

'He's not talking.'

'It's probably a throat infection,' she said. 'He's fine.'

Over the following week the stutter became worse and worse. By the end of it my brain had completely lost control of my voice and I fell totally silent, unable to form even single words like 'yes' or 'no' or 'help'. Mum thought at first that it was just me messing about and being difficult but eventually she had to admit that Wally might have a point and agreed to take me to see the doctor. Sitting in the surgery she related my story to him, giving it all the necessary drama and pathos to make it clear that she was really the one who was suffering the most, having lost her husband and been left with six children to bring up.

'The poor boy was there to witness it,' she told him, her voice catching on the tears she was pretending to swallow back. 'He saw his lovely father going up in flames in front of his eyes, just a few weeks ago. The two of them were so close, it's hit him hard.'

The doctor examined me and listened to everything she had to say and then explained what he thought had happened.

'I believe Joe has been struck mute from the shock of what he's witnessed,' he said gently.

He was obviously as concerned about upsetting her as he was about whatever was wrong with me.

'William was such a good husband and father,' she started up again. 'This is a tragedy for the whole family, but especially for Joe. And now my little boy has been struck dumb as well. How long will it be before he can talk again and get back to his normal self?'

'It could just be a short-term condition,' the doctor said doubtfully, obviously not having a clue. 'Or it could be a long-term problem. We'll just have to see how things develop.'

By the time we left the surgery the penny had dropped in Mum's head that I actually had become mute, and it wasn't just an act. She was partly annoyed with me for causing her yet more inconvenience and for trying to draw more attention to myself, but I suspect there was a part of her brain that was already beginning to see the possibilities, even at that stage. If I couldn't talk, I couldn't tell any tales.

It would be four and a half years before I was able to speak properly again and by striking me mute my brain had finally delivered me completely into Mum's power. I was totally helpless. Now that I couldn't speak, my frustration grew even greater, exploding out into uncontrollable physical tantrums and I started hitting furniture, throwing things and kicking doors in my silent rages. I didn't realize it, but the worse I behaved the more I was playing into Mum's hands, proving just what a difficult child I was and what a wonderful woman she was to be bringing me up on her own, especially when she had so many other children to care for at the same time.

Mum actually seemed to enjoy violence, relishing watching it almost as much as she relished doling it out herself. She used to rig up a sort of boxing ring in the second lounge at the house and make my three oldest brothers fight each other, with her as their coach and cheerleader as well as their audience. The room was not as smart as the rest of her home since she displayed all her best furniture in the other lounge. It was a part of the house that no one from outside the family would ever be invited into. It contained just an old fire and a tatty settee and chair. It would have been a comfortable 'family room' if we had been the kind of happy family to have such a thing. It was certainly a place where Mum could relax and unwind and not worry if there was some blood spilled on the carpet. There were always curtains drawn across the windows, with nets pulled tight behind them for extra protection against prying eyes. Even if she opened the windows to let in some air she still wouldn't part the curtains, not wanting anyone from the outside world to be able to glimpse into her private fiefdom and witness what she was getting up to. When she felt like some entertainment she would sit down in that room with a cup of tea, pushing the older boys on and on like gladiators in Ancient Rome, until one of them drew blood.

'Go on,' she'd jeer at them, 'punch him! Fucking kill him!'

If they tried to refuse they would get a beating from her, which would be far worse than anything they could do to each other. It didn't matter if they were really hurt, she would insist they continued to fight until blood had been spilled, beating them with a garden cane if they tried to stop. She couldn't allow any disobedience, couldn't show a single moment of weakness or kindness in case it undermined the terror that she relied on in order to reign supreme over us all. Once one of them was bleeding she would allow him to come out of the ring and she would bring in another to take on the winner. She would tell them that she was just trying to teach them how to fight, toughening them up so they would be able to look after themselves in the outside world, but it seemed more like she did it to indulge her own blood-lust. The only person they really needed to protect them-selves from was their own mother.

Most of the violence in the house was inflicted directly by her. If any of us dared to disobey her, or even just looked at her in the wrong way, she would immedi-ately lay into us in a blind rage. Sometimes she wouldn't even need to have a reason; she would just become angry and take it out on whoever was nearest. She would grab Thomas and me by the hair and literally swing us round by it until our feet lifted off the ground, sending us hurtling into the walls. Her strength sometimes seemed superhuman. If she didn't manage to get a satisfying lift-off first time she would repeat the manoeuvre until she got it right.

As part of her hard-done-by widow act, Mum successfully sued the garage for several thousand pounds in compensation for Dad's death, and Graeme closed the business down soon afterwards. Dad's best friend Derek felt so guilty about not being able to save Dad when the flames were engulfing him that he wrote a suicide note and drove his car off the motorway, killing himself in the crash. It seemed as though the repercussions from that little gust of wind were going to go on forever, like ripples on a pond disturbed by a stone.

Mum was determined to crush my spirit and put a stop to my disruptive behaviour once and for all and she beat me up so violently, so often, that I finally understood I must never question her or so much as look at her directly again. She was constantly warning me that next time I annoyed her she would kill me and as I lay on the floor in a battered heap I had no reason to doubt her. She made no effort to hold back the full force of her strength when she hit out; there was no self-control, no fear of causing damage, no worries about killing someone. It had become normal for me to be punched in the head or kicked over and over again for no reason at all. Even if I was behaving myself I still drove her mad, just because I was there and because I reminded her of the humiliation Dad and Marie had put her through.

The fact that I was now virtually silent, making only little squeaking noises instead of speaking, seemed to fuel her annoyance even further. It was as if she believed I was mocking her with my whimpering, my pleading eyes and frantically shaking head as I tried to dissuade her from hitting me any more. As far she was concerned I was no longer a human being; I had degenerated into a hated animal to be kicked and punched and abused at every opportunity, like a beaten dog slinking around in the shadows with its head down and eyes to the floor.

When I first lost my voice I found other ways to communicate. If I wanted something I would point at it and grunt and even that would drive her mad and so soon I stopped communicating at all. She made no secret of the fact that she detested me more and more every day; nothing I could have done would have made any difference by that stage.

'Don't fucking point,' she would snarl, giving me such a hard slap I would be knocked off my feet.

'Don't fucking look at me!'

'You smell fucking terrible!'

Everything was an excuse to hit me. It went on and on and on. She channelled every ounce of anger and disappointment she felt towards the world in general and my father in particular, and took it out on me. She would encourage the others to do the same and Larry and Barry were happy to cooperate, delighted to have someone so much further down the family pecking order than themselves. They always wanted to do things to please her, and they soon learned that any humiliation they wanted to inflict on me would earn her approval as well as satisfying their own sadistic instincts.

I was still sleeping on the floor in Larry and Barry's room. Wally had his own room at the top of the house and Thomas and Ellie shared another room. I would have much preferred to have been in with them but I knew better than to argue with any decision Mum made. I had to stay in the bedroom all day long, except at meal-times, but I wasn't allowed to play with anything in there that belonged to my brothers. If I so much as touched one of their belongings I would be given a beating and I had nothing of my own to play with. The boredom of just sitting there all day long increased the feelings of isolation and frustration that were building up inside me, until I was just itching to break out into mischief or destruction but never daring to.

At night I had no mattress or pillow, only a single blanket. Larry and Barry shared a double bed and resented having me in the house as much as Mum did. They bullied me at every opportunity and whenever they made a noise that disturbed Mum they would make sure I took the blame. She used to put us all to bed by six or seven in the evening so that she could have some solitary drinking time for herself. We would usually be awake again at four or four thirty, itching to get up and move about. Larry and Barry would start messing around together, fighting in bed and farting on each other, and if they woke Mum up she would shout through the wall.

'Shut the fuck up!'

'It's Joe,' they would yell back. I would open my mouth to protest my innocence, terrified of the punishment I would inevitably receive, but no sound would come out and Larry and Barry would giggle triumphantly as they waited for the entertainment that would follow.

Furious at being woken and at the thought that I would dare to play up after all she had done to tame me, she would come storming in and give me another beating. The fact that I had no voice with which to plead my innocence was probably irrelevant as I doubt she would have believed me anyway.

Larry and Barry were thick as thieves and they used to order me to do things that they knew would get me into trouble. Being five, brimming with repressed energy and boredom, and eager to please my big brothers to avoid getting a beating from them, I was easily influenced and always ended up being the one who got caught. Whenever there was any trouble Mum would blame me anyway, even if it was obvious it couldn't have been anything to do with me.

'None of this ever happened till you came on the scene,' she'd say about some minor infringement of her rules, and then she'd give me another battering, dragging me around by the hair with my mouth stretched open but the screams refusing to form in my throat.

One dark morning, just a few months after Dad died, Mum had finally had enough of me disturbing her sleep. She pulled me all the way down the stairs by my hair, shouting at the top of her voice.

'This time you have gone too fucking far, you little bastard. You've pushed me too far. I'm finished with being patient with you. I've fucking had enough!'

I really believed that she was finally going to kill me. She'd told me often enough that she would do it one day.

There was a door under the stairs, which I had assumed led to a broom cupboard; I had never seen anyone opening it and no one had ever mentioned what lay behind it but I would be finding out soon enough. Dragging me behind her along the hall floor, Mum threw open the under-stairs door. I saw another staircase stretching down into the darkness below and I felt a terrible foreboding of what might be in store. Was this where she took people she was going to kill?

She punched a light switch and I saw for the first time what I would later understand was a basement. This was nothing like the clean, orderly world of the rooms in the rest of the house. There was a smell of mustiness and damp rising up from the shadows thrown by the single light bulb. Thick cobwebs clung to the rough brick walls and bare wood. She hurled me down the stairs, kicking and punching as she followed me down. At the bottom there was another door, a big solid Victorian timber one, which she opened and threw me through with one last mighty slap, as if I was no more than a sack of straw. She turned on another light and I could see the full horror of where she was putting me.

Inside was a cellar containing nothing but a filthy old mattress propped up against the wall. Unable to stand the sight of me for a second longer she slammed the door shut behind me and switched off the light from the outside. I could hear her jamming something under the door handle so I wouldn't be able to get out. Then she stamped back up the stairs and there was silence as well as blackness.

For a moment it felt as though I was in total darkness, but as my eyes adjusted the few thin rays of light which filtered in through an airbrick high up in the wall once dawn broke gave me just enough vision to grope my way around. Even if she hadn't jammed the door I knew better than to try to open it without her permission in order to reach the light switch. The cold began to creep into my bones and I just sat shivering in the dark, wearing only my underpants, waiting to see what would happen next. I listened to the trains rumbling past outside the airbrick, wishing I could climb into one of the warm, bright carriages I had seen passing so many times and travel as far as possible from that room.

I had entered a world I hadn't even known existed a few minutes before; one that was to become my prison cell for the next three years.

Chapter Six

Incarceration

I don't think that Mum had any long-term plan to turn that dark little underground room into my prison cell at the moment she first pushed me in there and wedged the door shut. There was no lock on the door at that stage; that came later, which suggests she hadn't pre-planned my imprisonment. I think she had just had enough of me that morning – enough of what she saw as my spoiled, disruptive behaviour. She wanted to get me out of the way and teach me a lesson once and for all. It was only once I was in the cell that she realized it was the best place for me. She had accidentally found a way to keep me completely out of her sight, while keeping me available to vent her bitterness and anger on when it became too much to contain. She could keep me there for as long as she liked because there was no one she had to answer to.

When a child disappears it is usually their panicking and grief-stricken loved ones who raise the alarm, but in my case in was my loved ones who had caused me to vanish, so why would anyone else notice? The other people who might have cared what happened to me, like Marie and Aunt Melissa, had been chased away by Mum right from the beginning. They wouldn't have expected to hear anything from me.

While other children played outside in the sun, went to school, made friends and learned new things, I sat in the dark on my own. As far as I know, during those three years no one from social services asked where I was or what was happening to me. Perhaps they did come knocking and Mum managed to convince them with some story or other. Maybe she told them I had moved from the area, but I think they would have asked to see at least some evidence of where I was now to back up any claims she made. My name must have been on the system because I had been to see the local doctor when I first went mute, so I must have had a national health number at the very least. I'm also fairly sure Mum would have been collecting benefits for looking after me from the welfare because she needed every penny she could scrounge together. So how could I just have slipped out of sight like that without anyone questioning it? Maybe they were confused because I had been living at two different addresses – both Mum's and Marie's. Maybe their case load was just too great. I don't know and I suppose I'll never find out now.

After a while of sitting on the bare floor that first day, straining my ears as I listened out for her to come back down the stairs and give me another beating, I found the courage to stand up and pull the mattress flat onto the floor in order to give myself somewhere more comfortable to lie. I almost choked on the stale, damp stink that rose into the air on a cloud of dust as it dropped down, filling my lungs and making me wheeze. It was a relief to get my skinny limbs off the cold, hard concrete even though the mattress was full of lumps and sharp edges.

As I lay, staring up into the darkness, it wasn't long before I felt the approaching urge to pee. I hadn't emptied my bladder since the previous evening and I realized it was now painfully full. I had no idea how long I was going to be down there and I certainly didn't have the nerve to bang on the door for help or to even try to push my way through it and find my way back up the stairs in the dark. Knowing how angry she always became when I peed myself by mistake, I tried to hold it in but the pain eventually became so intense I had to give up and I released it onto the floor, knowing, even as the feeling of release spread through me, that I would be in trouble if she spotted the puddle. I hoped she wouldn't come back down before it evaporated, but in my heart I knew that was unlikely. The urine left a new smell in the air and although it was a relief to have got rid of it I felt even dirtier as I lay back down on the mattress again to wait for something to happen, wondering if perhaps this was the end and I was just going to be left alone to die of hunger and thirst.

Hours later I heard footsteps on the stairs and the light came on in the cell, almost blinding me with its sudden brightness. When Mum opened the door and came in I saw immediately from her expression that she could smell what I'd done and I cringed, bracing myself for the blows.

'You dirty little shit,' she growled, her lips curling up in disgust. 'You're not even fucking house trained.'

Just as I expected she went completely mental at me for daring to soil her house, even this distant, dirty, forgotten corner of it. Armed with a new reason to be angry, she pulled me up off the mattress by the hair and beat me hard. Still gripping my hair tightly she pushed me onto my knees and smeared my face into the puddle of wee with all her strength, as if she was trying to teach a particularly stubborn puppy the error of its ways, forcing me down so hard I was afraid she would break my nose.

'You dirty little bastard!' she screamed as she rubbed, before shouting up to Wally.

'Fetch a fucking mop and bucket!'

When Wally came hurrying down she hurled the mop at me with all her strength.

'Clean it up now,' she ordered.

She watched as I worked, shouting orders at me all the time: 'Scrub harder! Use more water!' Then she turned back to Wally.

'Get two more buckets of cold water,' she told him and he dutifully went back upstairs to dispose of the dirty water. I assumed she was going to use the fresh water to rinse down the floor, but once he had brought the buckets back down she sent him away and then threw the contents of both over me. The coldness of the water knocked the breath out of me.

'You stink,' she snarled. 'You dirty little bastard!'

She left one of the empty buckets behind for me to use as a toilet from then on and wedged the door handle from the other side as she left me alone in the dark once more, shivering on the soaking wet mattress and feeling utterly alone. What was going to become of me? Would I die of cold or of hunger first?

To start with, one of them would bring me food once a day most days, but the longer I was down there the more angry Mum seemed to become towards me and the less willing she was to put herself out to feed me. She saw me as nothing more than an inconvenience and a blight on her life and preferred to put me out of her mind. Sometimes it would be her who would bring the scraps down and sometimes she would send Larry and Barry, who were enjoying this new opportunity to humiliate me further. As far as they were concerned, the family dog was now being confined to a cage, which meant they didn't have to have me stinking up their bedroom any more. Once they realized that the worse they treated me the happier Mum would be with them, they exploited every new opportunity to indulge their hatred of me and their own sadistic impulses. Just as before they would spit in my food and throw it on the floor, forcing me to lick it up like a dog, which was a hundred times worse when it was the filthy dirty bricks of the cellar floor that I was having to lick rather than Mum's pristine kitchen floor. If I refused to do anything they ordered me to do they would call Mum.

'Joe has had one of his tantrums, Mum,' they'd say. 'He's thrown his food all over the floor. What should we do?'

She would then come clattering down the stairs and batter me and grind my face into it to teach me a lesson for being so disrespectful and ungrateful. When they brought down water in bottles it often tasted funny so I have no idea what they had put in it, and sometimes they would glue the tops onto the bottles so I would have to gnaw through the plastic just to get anything out of them. My baby teeth soon became so weak from malnutrition and lack of cleaning that they would chip and break under any sort of strain. Toothache was added to the long list of different kinds of pain I suffered from. In the end I didn't care how much it hurt or what the water tasted like because I was so thirsty I would have drunk anything.

Sometimes Mum even took away my underpants because she said I'd soiled them – 'You dirty little bastard. You need to be taught a lesson!' – then I was left naked for days. She fitted a bolt to the outside of the door so she didn't have to keep on wedging it every time she went in or out, which meant there was no chance of me ever getting out on my own. Sometimes when no one had been down for a day or two I would wonder what would happen if they completely forgot about me. Would I just be a skeleton on the mattress when they finally remembered to come and check on me? I would still have preferred to keep quiet and die in peace rather than bang on the door to remind them I was there because of all the wrath and pain that would bring down on my head.

Often when Mum was punishing me for something she would talk about Dad, punctuating her blows and kicks with verbal tirades.

'He was a rotten fucking man and a rotten fucking husband. And you are just as fucking bad as him.'

The pain he had caused her never seemed to fade; if anything it seemed to enrage her even more as time passed. It was as though he was becoming more of an obsession with her now that he was dead than he had been when he was alive. Maybe it angered her to think that he had escaped from her by dying, that she couldn't do anything to make his life a misery any more, so she turned her frustrations onto me instead.

'Every time I look at you it reminds me of that sick bastard!' she would say as she gave me another round of punches.

I still found myself thinking about him all the time as well, remembering our times together and wishing with all my heart that he was still alive. During the hours and hours that I sat alone in that cell I would chat to Dad in my head, just as I used to chat out loud when we were together in the car or the garage. I could picture him sitting on the mattress beside me, talking back to me. When my limbs got too stiff or cold, I would get up and pace around, trying to stretch them out, and pretending I was going for a walk with Dad. I went through a whole range of emotions in those days. Sometimes I was cross with him for being so careless with his own life and leaving me with Mum and the others when he knew that I needed his protection. Sometimes I just sank into black, total misery. What I wanted most was to die so that I could be with him all the time.

'I'm a good boy, God,' I would pray. 'Please take me too. Please let me be with my dad.'

I would fantasize sometimes. I would imagine so hard that I had a nice mummy and daddy who were both alive and both loved me and we all lived together in a happy family that the pictures in my head would seem almost real. These fantasies passed the time for a while but I would then come back to reality out of my daydreams with a sick feeling in my stomach as I realized it had all been in my mind and that I was still lying on my own in the dark, freezing cold and hungry.

Sometimes Mum and the others would leave me alone for so long the bucket I was supposed to use as a toilet would fill right to the top. When it had reached the brim I would hold my wee in for as long as I could bear, for fear of making it overflow onto the floor and having my face rubbed in it, but eventually I would have no choice but to give in. The stench from the bucket grew so overpowering that anyone coming into the cell would gag and cover their mouths and noses, reinforcing the idea that I was a filthy, stinking creature, no better than a caged animal in need of regular mucking out and sluicing down. Once the bucket was completely full and standing in a growing puddle, I would try to find new places that I thought would disguise the wetness, but it never fooled her for a second and I always ended up with my face being rubbed in it again.

One day, after I had been under the house for a few months, Mum made a surprise announcement. 'You stink so bad,' she told me, 'it's coming up through the floorboards. So you're going to have a fucking bath. Come on, get a fucking move on.'

She escorted me roughly and impatiently upstairs to the bathroom, cuffing me round the head as we went, and scrubbed me down herself with all the violence she could muster. I thought I heard a man's voice in the house while I was upstairs and when she escorted me back to the cellar again I found that someone had been in and fixed a proper lock to the door, one with a key that could be turned twice as if to finalize the locking in process once and for all. She must have got a locksmith in to do it. It was as though she was making my imprisonment official and my heart sank even further. Was I going to be kept there forever, until I died? It certainly looked that way.

As the months dragged on I grew accustomed to listening to the sounds outside the airbrick and in the house above. Sitting in the dark I had to rely on my ears for every bit of information and my hearing seemed to become more acute without any visual distractions. I would be able to tell who it was coming down to see me from the way they opened the top door and the speed and weight of their footsteps on the stairs. My worst fear was always that it would be Mum, because that invariably meant a beating, and the best times were when it was Wally being sent down with my food, or coming of his own accord to give me some company and comfort. He wasn't like the others and even though Mum would specifically tell him not to go down to see me when she went out, he would disobey her whenever he was sure he could get away with it.

Grown men might have gone insane when kept in solitary confinement as long as I was, particularly in such horrific conditions. I think the one thing that kept me from losing my mind was the visits from my oldest brother Wally. Even though Wally was eighteen years old by this stage, he was just as frightened of Mum's violence as everyone else and he always did what she told him, but he didn't enjoy being sadistic and bullying me the way the others did and whenever he thought she wouldn't find out he would be kind to me. I guess he was a bit of a geek, with his big thick Buddy Holly-style glasses, short hair and freckles and I loved him for those little kindnesses. He was the only good thing in my life during those long years.

When Mum was out at the pub and the others had been sent up to bed he would sometimes sneak down with a bit of stolen food for me and he would sit beside me on the stinking mattress and read stories from books about soldiers and young men, heroes and villains. Looking back, I think he made up some of those stories because they often seemed to be particularly relevant to my situation, fairy tales about evil mothers and little boys who eventually escaped and lived happily ever after. I think it was his way of giving me hope that things would get better one day; that my nightmare wouldn't go on forever. He used to treat me more like a grown-up than anyone else did. 'You're nearly seven now, Joe,' he'd say, 'it's time for you to be brave and strong.'

I knew he was right because that was what all the stories he read to me were about, young boys being heroes in the face of adversity and triumphing over evil, but I also thought it was easy for him to say when he had his freedom and a nice warm bedroom to go to when he wanted to escape the shouting and violence.

When it was just the two of us he would laugh about Mum, calling her 'the piss artist'. I didn't know what a piss artist was, and I didn't have the voice to ask him any questions, but I imagined it must be some sort of job she was doing. I reckoned she must be good at it and make a lot of money in order to be able to support so many of us.

Spending so much time on my own in the dark meant that my understanding of things like language and the way the outside world worked got more and more behind for my age. Wally was the only person who talked to me properly; the rest of them just swore at me and taunted me, so he was the only one teaching me anything worthwhile at all. But I couldn't ask him any questions, so even he could only teach me a limited amount. Sometimes he would manage to make me laugh inside my head and even though I made no sound he would be able to tell I was laughing because I would make the same little frowning expression every time. This would set him off laughing too and for a few minutes I would be happy and able to forget all the pain and misery.

'Mum's a bit doolally in the head,' he would tell me, but I didn't know what that meant. I looked at him, confused. 'You know, cuckoo,' he searched for a better way to explain it. 'Nuts in the head!'

I tried to imagine how anyone could get a cuckoo and nuts inside their head. He'd often told me she was ill in the head, so maybe it was the cuckoo and the nuts that were causing the illness. Small children learn almost everything in life by asking questions of adults. When you aren't able to do that, when you sometimes have no one with you at all for days on end and no mental stimulation, it must do something to a young, developing brain. It certainly slowed down my development in those years, stunting my ability to make sense of the world around me and to understand things that other children my age would have taken for granted. I was living in a vacuum, cut off from all normal life with no mental stimulation beyond Wally's fleeting visits.

He would try to encourage me to speak, patiently attempting to extract even the simplest sounds from my apparently paralysed voice box, constantly trying to restore the confidence that the others had battered out of me.

'One day you're going to grow up to be very intelligent,' he would tell me. 'That means clever.'

I actually doubted if I would grow up at all because Mummy was always telling me I would be dead before my next birthday, but I still liked to be flattered and to think that someone believed in me and believed that there would eventually be an end to my suffering and an escape from my cell.

Sometimes Wally would play tricks on me, though. On the first of April one year he came downstairs and told me that Mum had fallen downstairs and died. I felt as though a weight was lifting off my heart. I was free and God had answered all my prayers. When Wally told me that it was April Fools' Day and he was only joking it was as though the whole world had landed back on my shoulders again.

'You aren't that lucky, Bro,' he said before leaving the cell again. 'But maybe one day your time will come.'

One evening when he visited, I couldn't stop shaking and he explained to me that it was my body recovering from the shock of the beating Mum had given me an hour or two before. Every part of me used to hurt after those beatings. Once my heart was racing so fast Wally said he was worried I was going to explode. I must have looked panicked when he said that because he laughed at the expression on my face.

'Don't worry,' he said. 'I won't let that happen.'

He was always terrified of being caught down there without permission and so he would sneak off again after what seemed to me like just a few minutes. If he heard Mum's footsteps going past on the path outside the airbrick he would know he just had enough time to get back upstairs before she managed to get round the house and open the front door with her key. She would nearly always be rolling drunk by then, back from the pub and shouting obscenities at the top of her voice at anyone who was in the house. That would help to slow down her progress and Wally could tell exactly where she was from the noise. I would be desperate not to be left alone in the dark again and would cling to Wally's leg like a frightened toddler, staring up at him with imploring eyes, whimpering like a puppy.

'You don't want your brother getting in trouble, do you?' he would say as he struggled to get away from me. 'You've got to let me go now, Joe.'

In the end he would have to peel me off and force me back so he could get out the door, hurriedly pushing me in so he could lock it behind him before turning out the lights and rushing up the stairs.

It was usually him who would take my toilet bucket up to empty, but he was only allowed to do that if Mum had told him to. If she caught him doing anything for me out of kindness he would be in trouble himself. Wally had explained to me that he would sometimes have to pretend to be nasty to me if Mummy or the other boys were around. He explained that it was in my interests to keep the charade up, as well as his. 'If she thinks I'm being nice to you,' he explained, 'she won't let me down here to see you any more and I won't be able to help you at all.'

One night he felt so bad for me he tried to sneak down at two in the morning with a load of cakes when he thought Mum had gone to bed – but she caught him before he could get through the top door. I could hear her shouting from where I was lying.

'What the fuck are you doing at this time of night? Where are you going with all those?'

'It's nothing. I was just going to tease him a bit,' he lied, 'and eat them in front of him.'

She can't have believed him because I could hear him being beaten for that and I convinced myself that it was all my fault for making him feel sorry for me.

If it hadn't been for Wally's secret visits I think I would have died of starvation or just gone completely insane in those months and years. They were the only thing I had to look forward to, the only relief from the loneliness and agony of my existence. I'm convinced that without his kindness I wouldn't have survived.

* * *

I never knew when another beating from Mum was coming. Sometimes she'd forget about me for days on end, and at other times my punishments would be more regular. There were evenings when she tried to get at me after she came back from the pub, in the mood for giving me a beating, but she would be too drunk to get the key into the cellar door. I would be huddled on the mattress, shaking with fear as I listened to her on the other side, banging around, swearing and shouting about how she was going to kill me, telling me what a little bastard I was and how I would be sorry once she got her hands on me. It was always a relief to hear her finally giving up and stumbling back up the stairs, because then I would know I was safe from her for at least a few hours while she slept off the effects of the drink.

After I had been in the cellar for a few months, not content with giving me arbitrary beatings, Mum decided she should make my punishments more formalized, more like rituals. She got Larry and Barry to bring three solid old wooden chairs down to the cell, and the three of them would strip me naked and stretch me across them. My brothers held my wrists and ankles while Mum beat me viciously with bamboo canes that they had stolen from the nearby allotments, or with a broomstick.

'You no-good little bastard,' she would shout as she hit me over and over again. 'I fucking hate you! If I had a gun I would shoot you dead.'

Larry and Barry would be laughing all the time and egging her on. 'Give it to him, the little twat!'

I wanted to scream but no sound would come out; all the pain stayed locked in my brain instead. In the end I would pass out during those beatings. I'd wake up a while later to find I had been chucked back onto the mattress, every part of me aching, fighting for breath and hardly able to move.

One time when I woke up I found that I wasn't lying down as usual. While I had been unconscious my wrists had been tied above my head to a piece of iron piping that ran from the floor to the ceiling. I was still naked and the whole surface of my back was in agonizing pain from the beating I had just received. A bucket of cold water suddenly hit me, bringing me fully back to consciousness. I gasped, trying desperately to pull enough air into my lungs to breathe, wheezing and rasping. Mum was laughing at me, still holding the empty bucket.

'Nothing to say for yourself, you little bastard?' she asked. 'Where's your rotten fucking father now when you need him?'

I managed to lift my head and looked into her eyes. I immediately realized it was a mistake to make eye contact and averted them again but it was too late to stop her lunging at me, grabbing hold of my hair and smashing the back of my head into the pipe behind me.

'Don't look at me like that, you little shit!'

I bit my tongue and tasted the blood in my mouth. I remember thinking that if I had a gun I would shoot myself between the eyes rather than have to take any more of this. Mum then stormed out of the cell and I heard her banging her way angrily up the stairs. My whole body was trembling uncontrollably and I must have passed out again from the pain.

The next thing I knew I was jerked awake by the sound of someone coming back down the stairs. Oh no, I thought, not again. There was too much noise in my head and ringing in my ears to be able to work out who it might be. Surely this time she would actually kill me as she was always promising and finally put me out of my misery. I must have tipped her too far over the edge by daring to look at her, making her think I was being insolent. I was fighting for breath and I could feel tears trickling down my cheeks as the key turned twice in the lock.

'It's okay, Joe,' Wally said. 'It's only me.' He looked at me with such sad eyes. 'Why do you wind her up?' he asked kindly. 'What have I told you about not looking at her, you silly boy? Always look at the floor when she's talking to you.'

She must have given him permission to come down and release me because he untied my wrists from the pipe and I know he would never have dared to do it of his own accord. My arms slumped down and I fell onto the hard, cold floor as if I was dead. He gently massaged my wrists to try to get the blood flowing through them again, then lifted me under the arms and eased me across the floor onto the mattress, lying me down on my front as carefully as he could.

'This is all your Dad's fault, you know,' he said as he gently bathed my wounds with salt water, but I couldn't be bothered to listen any more. I was hurting too much and I was bored with hearing the same things over and over again, even from Wally. 'This is going to hurt a bit,' he warned me and I scrunched my face up as the salt went into the cuts. It felt good to have him tending to me so gently, even if the salt did sting. After a while he stood up to go, telling me to lie quietly until he was able to get back. I heard the door being locked again and the light went out. Then his footsteps disappeared up the stairs. I had to drag myself to the poo bucket to be sick and in the dim light of the airbrick I thought I could see streaks of blood in the vomit. I didn't have the strength to crawl back to the mattress so I just laid my head down on the concrete and slipped back into a merciful unconsciousness.

The next time I was woken it was by Larry crashing into the cell.

'Hi, shit face,' he said, slapping me painfully on the back. 'Oh sorry,' he laughed, 'forgot you were sore there. Enjoy the lemonade, dickhead!'

He chucked a large plastic bottle onto the floor beside me and it wasn't until he'd gone and I tried to open it that I realized they had glued the top on before bringing it down. I didn't have the strength to gnaw it off straight away; instead I drifted into unconsciousness again.

Mum would leave those three hard chairs in the cell to remind me what was in store for me soon, as if I could ever forget. I just wished I could find my voice so that I could tell her how sorry I was that Daddy had let her down so badly. I wished there was something I could say or do to make her stop hating me so much but, if anything, her anger seemed to get fiercer as the days went by. Because I was so run down, and constantly breathing the damp, stale, fetid air of the cellar, I started to develop asthma. I was always fighting for breath, particularly when I was afraid, which was most of the time. The wheezing noises I made when I was trying to pull enough air into my lungs was another source of annoyance to Mum, another reason to give me a slap, which in turn made me struggle all the more for breath. There was nothing I could do. I was utterly and completely powerless.

I usually had no way of telling how long I had been down in the cellar but I knew the day that it was my seventh birthday because Larry and Barry came crashing down the stairs, flashing the light in the cell on and off from the outside and shouting, 'Happy birthday, bastard! Are you ready for a surprise, you little wanker?' They burst through the door laughing uncontrollably and I knew what was coming next because they'd done it to me before. I wasn't excited, just scared.

'You don't deserve any presents,' Mum told me as she came into the cell behind them, 'because you're the child of a deceitful, cheating, dead bastard.'

Each birthday my brothers always gave me the hardest birthday bumps possible and this year was no exception. They threw me as high as they could and let me drop to the concrete floor while Mum watched approvingly. They grabbed me by the arms and legs as I frantically shook my head to let them know that I didn't like it but they pretended not to understand.

'Speak up if you want them to stop,' Mum said, knowing, of course, that I couldn't.

The shock of the falls to the floor left me completely winded.

Just as they finished, I saw Wally coming in carrying a present.

'Happy birthday, Bro,' he said, gently placing the present in my trembling hands.

I looked at it in horror. What on earth was he doing? Was it a joke? Why would he give me a present while Mum was watching? He must have known what the reaction would be.

Mum snatched it away and threw it against the wall with all her strength, smashing whatever was inside. I heard a breaking sound. Swinging round she slapped Wally hard in the face, screaming abuse at him for daring to be kind to me when he knew it wasn't allowed, that I didn't deserve it, that I needed to be punished and taught a lesson.

'Calm down, Mum,' he said, thinking quickly. 'It was just a joke. I was just teasing him, to piss him off. I was hoping you would do the honours and smash it against the wall in front of the little bastard.'

It was the most unconvincing lie I had ever heard Wally utter. I couldn't believe he was going to get away with it, but Mum immediately stopped shouting at him and started apologizing for smacking him instead.

'Sorry, son,' she said, smiling at him sweetly. 'You know how I get sometimes. The little bastard don't deserve fuck all! Let him rot.' She lunged towards me, screaming into my ear. 'Look what you've made me do to my Wally, you little bastard.'

I kept my eyes glued to the floor, terrified to look up so I didn't see the kick coming until it connected with my head. She picked up the broken present, turned and stormed out of the cell, ordering Larry and Barry to go with her and telling Wally to lock the door after him.

Once I could hear they had gone, I glanced up at Wally and he winked at me, but I saw the tears welling in his eyes, magnified by his thick glasses. 'Sorry,' he mouthed before backing out the room and locking the door as he had been told.

I didn't blame him for lying. I knew he was as frightened of her as I was. I was surprised that he had even taken the risk of bringing me a present at all and I doubted he would make that mistake again. It felt as though Mum had broken a few more of my teeth with her kick. I remembered my grandfather used to keep his teeth in a glass beside his bed and put them in when he got up in the morning and I wondered if I'd be able to get false teeth like his once mine were all gone. But the idea of putting those horrible plastic things in my mouth made me shiver.

I sat cuddling myself on the mattress for a few hours, trying to conserve my body heat, when I heard footsteps again and my heart started to race, making my breathing difficult. Was I in for another beating? The key turned and it was Larry.

'There you go, dick. I got some yummy scraps for you,' he grinned, holding out the dog bowl. 'Sorry we ate your birthday cake, weren't enough left for you. If you beg nicely I might not gob in it.'

I was starving so I looked up at him in a sorrowful way, like a dog would. He burst out laughing and spat into the bowl anyway before tipping it all over me.

'I've added some extra flavours,' he shouted as he left the cell again.

The scraps were covered in salt and pepper, making them nearly inedible, making me heave on every mouthful, but I was so hungry I forced myself to keep eating. If I didn't eat something the pains in my stomach would grow worse, so I didn't have a choice.

The months went by and I kept myself going somehow. I'd pace round the cell when my muscles got too stiff, I'd daydream about Dad or about my ideal family, and, above all, I'd strain my ears for Wally's footsteps on the stairs, hopefully bringing me some food and a little bit of human kindness.

One day he told me some news, that he'd got himself a girlfriend. My initial reaction was to think 'A girlfriend! Yuk!' I didn't like the idea at all. I knew I would never get to meet her because no one in their right mind would ever bring a girlfriend into a place as terrible as my cell. Mum would never allow it anyway. I doubted if she even allowed the girl into the house, fearful of what she might see and who she might tell. Not that Wally would have been in a hurry to bring her. How could he show a girl what his family did to his little brother and expect her to just say nothing? He was probably frightened he would lose her if she found out too much. He can't have been proud of the fact that his family kept a small boy prisoner in the cellar. I could understand all that, but I would still have liked to meet her.

I didn't realize the implications at the time, but over the next few months his visits to the cellar became less frequent. I guess he must have been out of the house more often, round at her place probably. Anywhere else would be a better place to be if you had a choice. But it meant that my existence became even more wretched without the comfort he brought.

Sometimes I'd just lie on the mattress and cry for hours on end. No sound came out except for a faint whimpering, but my whole body shook with grief, my chest ached and my throat closed up. It felt as though I was being crushed by a giant weight pressing down on me. In those moments, I lost all hope. I truly believed that this was what my miserable life would be like, day after agonizing day, until Mum finally did as she kept promising to do and killed me.

Chapter Seven

Mum's New Boyfriend

I think it must have been about eighteen months after I was first banished to the cellar, not long after my seventh birthday, when things changed upstairs in the house. Mum was still waging a one-woman war against Dad and his family, determined to extract every ounce of revenge possible even though Dad was dead. She must have met Aunt Melissa's husband Amani in the pub and spotted her opportunity to take one last kick at Dad's memory by seducing him and trying to break up his marriage.

The first I knew about this new twist to our family relationships was one evening when I had my ear pressed to the cellar door, attempting to hear what was going on in the house. I did this sometimes in order to help pass some time. As I listened, I heard Mum telling someone to bring me upstairs to her and quickly rushed back to my mattress in case they got angry with me for being nosey. The key was turned in the lock and Wally appeared, beckoning for me to follow him. It was such a rare occurrence that it was always exciting to be let out, even though as I pulled myself to my feet my heart was pounding with fear of what might be about to happen to me now. I hardly ever saw Mum without receiving at least one punch or kick, and usually she was unable to resist giving me a full-scale beating once she actually saw me and felt the familiar annoyance rising up inside her.

Wally rolled his eyes and murmured, 'The piss artist wants you.'

I followed him up the steps and he stood me next to Thomas, who was already lined up in the passageway as if we were on parade. Wally then vanished out the front door, obviously not wanting to be around to watch if Mum started laying into us. I stood as still as I could possibly manage with my eyes on the floor, knowing that any movement I made or expression that crossed my face might trigger an explosion of anger. I was aware she was talking to us but I was having trouble focusing my brain on her words. I could see her lips moving and then suddenly she was screaming just a few inches from my ears, making them ring.

Out of the corner of my eye, I saw a figure I recognized. It was Amani, my uncle, married to Dad's sister.

Mum was telling us not to call him 'Uncle Amani' any more, that now we had to call him 'Daddy'.

'Why?' Thomas asked innocently and she slapped him hard round the face for daring to speak up.

His comment seemed funny to me and I wasn't able to stop a smile breaking through, which earned me a slap as well.

'Our daddy's dead,' Thomas went on defiantly. 'I don't want another dad.'

I glanced across at him, admiring his guts but wishing he had kept quiet. He was still only four and obviously hadn't learned how to look after himself in that house. Mum punched the door angrily and then punched Thomas in the face and told him to go to his room. As he scuttled away, clutching at his cheek, she grabbed me by the throat.

'Have you got anything to say to me?' she asked. I could feel her spit on my face.

I shook my head as best I could and closed my eyes as she punched me hard in the ear. She opened the door at the top of the cellar stairs and threw me to the bottom, the slap still ringing in my ears as I bounced down, banging into the walls, pursued by her shouts.

'Get back in your hole!'

I stumbled into the cell and pulled the door closed behind me then sank onto the mattress, the right-hand side of my body feeling bruised and broken where it had clattered off the steps. I felt sorry for Thomas as he was still upstairs with her. At moments like that I was almost glad of the sanctuary of my hole in the ground.

Then I felt a twinge of hope. Maybe Amani would turn out to be the one who would save me? Even though Dad, who got on with virtually everyone except Mum, hadn't liked him much, Amani had always been nice enough to me when I was at Aunt Melissa's house. I thought that once he found out what Mum was doing to me he would tell my aunt what was happening and together they would help me to escape. I remembered how fiercely Aunt Melissa used to fight with Mum in the garage and how scared of her Mum had seemed. If she came to my rescue maybe I stood a chance.

But when Amani came down to the cellar to see me later, he didn't look as though he was shocked by the state of me or feeling friendly towards me in any way. He was tall and ugly and scary-looking, with a large mole next to his thick, long nose. His skin was a dark black colour and his hair was thick and curly. As he walked in through the cell door he covered his nose with his gigantic hand because of the smell from me, from the mattress and from the bucket. I was used to that because everyone reacted the same way when they walked in; even Wally wasn't able to stop himself from retching sometimes. It seemed to make Mum and Larry and Barry hate me even more, confirming in their eyes that I was just some sort of filthy animal, making myself smell on purpose in some way just to annoy them.

Amani was puffing on a big cigar, which probably helped him to cope with the smell a bit better, and he looked at me as if I was a piece of dirt he'd found on the bottom of his shoe. I smiled cautiously, hoping that he was just pretending to hate me for Mum's benefit, like Wally always did, but there was no response in his eyes; he just looked disgusted.

I was shocked when he walked back out without saying a word, slamming and locking the door behind him. I still tried to convince myself that he would tell Aunt Melissa what was happening once he was safely out of the house and she would get me help, but it wasn't long before I discovered that rescuing me wasn't part of his plan at all. In those few moments that he stood staring at me in the cell, Amani had sensed an opportunity and he intended to make full use of it.

What I didn't realize was that he was the sort of guy who would have sex with anything or anyone he could. He was in our house to have sex with Mum and anyone else who was available and he wasn't about to let on to Melissa about his new arrangements unless he had to. He didn't care about my plight in the slightest; in fact seeing me in that cell had given him some different ideas of his own.

The next time he was able to get down to my cell, Wally told me a bit about our new 'stepfather'. He must have guessed I would be curious. It's not every day you get told you've got a new dad.

'Amani comes from Nigeria,' Wally said, but I didn't have any idea where Nigeria was. I thought it might be in Scotland, which was the only other country I'd ever really heard of. I raised my eyebrows to show I didn't understand.

'It's a very hot country,' he explained, 'far away from here, in Africa.' I wondered if it was the sun that had burnt his face in this hot country, making him such a different colour to me, a boy whose skin never got to see the light of day at all. 'They have elephants there, and giraffes and lions.' He also told me that Amani liked to smoke some kind of weed all day long and that I'd probably notice the funny smell sometimes.

Once Amani had found out that I was locked in the cellar and had no way of defending myself, and once he realized that Mum was happy for him to do whatever he wanted to me, and would sometimes even take pleasure herself from watching, he started to come downstairs quite regularly. I soon learned to dread the sound of his footsteps as much as I dreaded hers or Larry's or Barry's.

Sometimes he would come down on his own when the rest of the house was quiet. I guessed the others were all asleep while he was prowling around, but it was possible they all knew exactly what was happening even then, and didn't care. I would hear the door at the top of the stairs creaking open and I learned to distinguish his footfall just as I did with the others. As soon as I heard it I knew what to expect. I would keep my eyes tight shut, pretending to be asleep, but he wouldn't bother to put the light on in the cell, so I was wasting my time putting on any sort of act. He didn't care if I was awake or not. He would lie down beside me on the vile mattress, whispering into my ear that I was 'a good boy', sticking his hand down my pants if I was wearing any, and rubbing himself against me. The first time he did it I pushed him away and shook my head to tell him I didn't like it, that I wanted him to stop. Wally had once told me that no one had the right to touch me in my private areas, and I believed him so I struggled and tried to get away. Even in the dark Amani must have sensed that I was resisting him.

'Don't say no to me, boy,' he snarled, grabbing my private parts and twisting them painfully. I didn't dare say no again because I could tell he was just like Mum, not someone who was willing to be disobeyed, unconcerned by how much pain he had to inflict on others in order to get his own way. I longed to scream out loud but the sounds wouldn't come, so I just lay still and hoped he wouldn't hurt me too much.

'If you tell anyone about this I'll stab your eyes out and chop off your willy,' he would warn me after he'd finished. But he was wasting his threats because I couldn't speak so how was I going to tell anyone anything?

Since his arrival I'd been given a dirty fitted sheet to cover the mattress, and Amani would wipe himself on that, leaving a cold wet patch behind him. Then he would walk out of the room as if nothing had happened, locking the door again behind him.

I soon realized that he thought I was just there for his convenience and Mum was happy to encourage that idea. He and Mum enjoyed coming down to the cellar together and they both liked to make fun of me and tell me I was a waste of time and a waste of space. Amani quickly moved on from rubbing himself against me to getting me to perform sex acts on him. I didn't always understand what it was he wanted me to do and if I didn't do everything he told me to do properly when Mum was there they would both batter me together, seeming to enjoy the violence almost as much as the sexual relief. After the beating I would then have to do the act again properly and Mum would stay to watch. Once Amani had finished with me he would just throw me back down onto the mattress, call me a 'dirty little bastard', and they would go off upstairs together laughing happily.

I often used to guess in advance when Amani was likely to be coming to visit me because Wally would be sent down to empty the slops bucket and Mum would come in spraying air freshener around the place to try to make the air less chokingly disgusting. Not that any spray could make much difference when the stench was so ingrained into everything. I soon learned that there was never any point in trying to stop Amani doing what he wanted because he was a thousand times stronger than me. His hands were enormous and he would put them round my throat as he told me what to do, exerting just enough pressure to let me know he could squeeze the life out of me as easily as snapping a matchstick.

'If you don't do it right,' he'd say each time, 'I'll kill you.'

I was certain that he was capable of it. I already knew that they could do whatever they wanted to me and no one would ever come to save me, so why wouldn't they kill me too? No one else in the house would ever have the nerve to tell on them, not even Wally. Once I was dead I would be forgotten completely within a few days, but at least I would be with Dad and I would be free of all the pain.

'Mum and Amani are the masters,' Wally told me one day. 'They like to play mind games and you will have to stay strong to win against them.' I liked the idea of being some sort of mind games warrior, but I couldn't always be strong and usually my encounters with them left me feeling completely defeated.

Sometimes Amani would take me upstairs to the bathroom and make me get into the bath in front of him. He would lock the door and pull his trousers down. I remember on one of those occasions I caught sight of myself in the mirror and was horrified at the sight of my bones protruding through my skin and the haunted look in my eyes.

'Look at me,' Amani snapped, and then he stood there playing with himself. At first I tried to look away but he slapped my face hard. 'I said look at me! Don't make me mad or I'll fucking hurt you.'

Then he made me stand up and wash myself in front of him. I felt ashamed and dirty. No one had ever told me these things were wrong, but I felt it instinctively. Dad would never have done anything like this, never mind all the other disgusting things Amani made me do. It seemed as though every day he came to see me he had some new, horrible sex act in mind, and it wasn't long before he started raping me. It hurt so much at first that I passed out, and I'd be left bleeding afterwards and shaking in agony. I was frequently sick after his visits, and there was never time for me to heal between one rape and the next. It was a horrific new kind of torture that took me to new depths of despair.

Just when I thought I couldn't sink any lower, my last lifeline was taken away. One day Wally came down to see me and I could tell from his expression he had something important he wanted to tell me.

'I'm leaving,' he said.

He must have seen the expression of horror in my eyes because he looked away as though he felt guilty about what he was doing to me.

'I'm going to live with my girlfriend and finally get away from the piss artist.'

He had managed to find an escape route out of our family from hell and I envied him. I couldn't wait to be able to follow him, if I managed to live that long.

'I'll be coming back to get you as soon as I can,' he said. 'I promise I won't leave you here.'

I felt a surge of hope. If I could just stay alive for a few more weeks, I told myself, Wally would be back to rescue me and would take me to live with him and his nice girlfriend, and we would be like a happy family.

But the days passed and nothing happened. I waited and waited without any change in my circumstances, imagining that perhaps Wally was telling someone in the outside world about me. Surely they would soon come looking for me and would rescue me, battering down the doors and fighting off Mum and the other boys, like the cavalry galloping to the rescue? I imagined how shocked they would be when they found me and how they would feel sorry for me and want to help me, feeding me nice food and tucking me up in a clean, warm bed. A week went by and then another and it was a long time before my hope started to fade.

But I guess Wally never did tell anyone; or if he did then they didn't believe him. It would have sounded pretty far-fetched to have someone telling you that his mother was keeping his mute baby brother prisoner in a cellar, starving him and torturing him just for fun. I imagine also that even once he was out of the house he was still too frightened of Mum to do anything against her in case she came after him or did something to his girlfriend.

So Wally just disappeared out of my life and I never saw him again. I can imagine how relieved he was to escape from her, but how could he have left me to their mercy like that, knowing how they treated me? How could he have slept at night knowing that I was still down under the ground without a single ally in the house above?

'I'll look after you now,' Amani promised me and despite all the bad things he had done to me that still kindled a tiny spark of hope in my heart. 'I'll do a better job than Wally ever did. If you're a good boy you can have his bedroom.'

He promised me the bedroom so often over the following weeks that I became really excited about it. I couldn't stop smiling at the thought of sleeping in a comfortable bed and maybe even having some of Wally's old childhood toys to play with.

'If you do what I say we'll get on okay,' Amani assured me. I hoped that was true because he was my only chance now.

But it wasn't long before Mum decided who was going to have what room and put a stop to any dreams I might have had for leaving the cellar. Ellie and Thomas were moved into Wally's room and I stayed exactly where I was. Amani might have been a physically powerful man, but it was still Mum who was in charge. Not that he seemed to care because he was getting exactly what he wanted from our new family arrangement. He couldn't have been happier.

Chapter Eight

Rescued from the Cellar

I was kept imprisoned in the cellar for nearly three years, between the ages of five and eight, and no one from the outside world noticed that I had vanished off the face of the earth. Day after day I sat in the dark waiting for the next beating or the next rape, hunger and thirst constantly gnawing away at my insides, cold eating into my bones and asthma clogging my lungs. Once Wally had abandoned me no one showed me even a moment's kindness and the easiest times were when it was just me on my own, talking in my head to Dad, with the cellar door double-locked and my tormentors safely on the other side.

As far as I'm aware, no one from social services ever came to look for me. Maybe I'd slipped through the net in some kind of bureaucratic cock-up or maybe Mum spun them a line – I just don't know. No one noticed that

I hadn't been enrolled in any of the local schools either, until the day that Thomas mentioned to his teacher that he and Ellie had another older brother apart from Wally, Larry and Barry. Mum must have forgotten to make sure he understood he was never to mention me to anyone outside the house. Or maybe she had told him and Thomas was getting self-assured enough to disobey her a little from time to time.

'Have you?' the teacher was obviously surprised by the news. 'What's his name?'

'Joe,' Thomas told her innocently.

'What school does he go to?'

'He doesn't go to school.'

Puzzled, the teacher must have reported the conversation to the headmaster of the school, who then invited Mum in to talk about it.

'Thomas tells us you have another lad called Joe,' he said.

'Oh, yes,' she said, smart enough to know it would be pointless to deny it.

'Why,' he asked her, 'doesn't Joe go to school?'

'He has problems,' Mum told them, no doubt with a convincing look of pained martyrdom on her face. 'He's mute and he's very disruptive. He's got a tilted brain.'

'But why haven't you enrolled him in a school?' the headmaster persevered.

'He's very destructive,' she said, as if that answered everything. 'I couldn't inflict him on other people's children. No one can control him.'

I imagine Mum had to think quickly at this stage. She must have known that she could get into trouble for keeping me out of school for three years, but she probably thought that if she played up how difficult I was, it would make it look as though she had been shouldering the whole burden of looking after me, that she had been acting with noble intentions even if she had technically broken the law. Because I knew nothing about the world beyond what happened in my cell, my behaviour would bear out everything she said about me. They had been treating me like a caged wild animal for so long that I had become one and any school that took me on was going to have its work cut out introducing me into a class full of other children. Once the authorities had been alerted to my existence, however, they could not forget about me again.

'We will need to come and meet Joe,' the social services department told Mum when the surprising news was passed on to them, 'to assess his needs so we can work out how best to help him, and you.'

An appointment was duly made and the day that the welfare worker was due to come to the house to meet me I was brought up from the cellar and scrubbed down.

'You'd better behave yourself,' Mum warned as she got me ready, brushing my teeth for the first time in three years and dressing me roughly in some new clothes I had never seen before. 'Or I'm going to give you a right battering once she's gone.'

It felt strange to have clean, soft material next to my skin after so many years of shivering naked or in nothing more than my soiled underpants. Everything smelled so fresh and exotic.

Mum took me into her posh sitting room to wait. It was a room I had never even seen before and I was overawed with its immaculate decorations and furniture, having spent so long with nothing to look at but bare walls, floors and an old mattress. With Mum hovering around me like a bomb waiting to go off, I felt as though I had been brought into enemy territory and part of me would have liked to be back under the floorboards again, behind the safety of a double-locked door.

She gave me a glass of something to drink and my hand was shaking so much I was frightened I was going to spill it on the swirly-patterned green carpet. Mum had told me so often that I was going to be killed that I began to wonder if this was to be the day of my execution; was someone coming to take me away and kill me because I had been so much trouble to my mother and because my father had been so bad to her? Every time Mum came down to the cellar to beat me or make me do something

I would think that this time it was going to be my time to die. I was always surprised to find that I was still alive at the end of each ordeal.

'Stop shaking!' she ordered me and I tried my hardest by holding my wrist with my other hand.

I was so confused. I couldn't work out what her plan was or when I was going to be hit again. I got more and more scared of what was coming until my heart was racing. How would they kill me? Would it be agony? Would I go to hell when I died?

When the doorbell rang Mum took the glass back from me and placed it carefully on the coffee table before going out to let the welfare worker in, welcoming her into the house as though she was delighted to see her.

As I stood there, shaking, I could hear her talking outside in a sweet, reasonable voice she never used around the house when it was just family. 'Hello, do come in … How nice to meet you … It's so kind of you to come and see us … Come through and meet Joe.'

When she came back into the room she was smiling all over her face and treating me as though I was her most precious child.

'Sit down here, darling,' she crooned at me, pointing to the corner of her settee, something I had never been allowed to do before. I was terrified of what might be going to happen next as the woman I suspected might be my executioner entered the room behind her, looking deceptively friendly. As she came towards me the welfare worker held out her hand for me to shake.

'Hello, young man,' she said in a warm, kind voice.

Assuming I was about to be hit, because that was all I had known for the previous three years or more, I reacted instinctively to defend myself and bit her hand, instantly proving that everything Mum had told them about me being aggressive and disruptive was true. The woman screamed and my teeth stayed tightly clamped into her flesh. I didn't want to let go because as long as her hand was between my teeth she couldn't use it to hit me.

'I am so sorry,' Mum said, taking my face between her fingers. 'Come along Joe, let go now.'

I expected her to punch me in the ear like she normally would have done in such a situation and braced myself for the blow, but instead her touch was gentle and caring.

'Come on, darling,' she coaxed sweetly. 'Let go of the nice lady.'

When they finally prised my teeth open I started kicking and screaming, determined not to be taken to my execution without putting up a fight. I figured I had nothing left to lose now if they were going to kill me anyway. Mum restrained me, kindly but firmly. I dare say the welfare worker was impressed with her saintly maternal patience in the face of such provocation.

'I can see why you haven't enrolled him,' the woman said as she sat down on one of the chairs, nursing her wounded hand and eyeing me nervously in case I flew at her again.

'I can't let him mix with other children,' Mum said. 'Not when he's liable to behave like that.'

'I do see what you mean,' the woman assured her sympathetically, 'but I'm afraid he must go to school. It's the law. There's a lot we can do to help him, and to help you.'

Unable to speak up in order to defend myself in any way I had to listen while Mum did all my talking for me. Before he went away Wally had been trying to help me to talk but at that stage I had only just started to be able to form single sounds like 'aah' or 'the'. It was impossible to communicate anything with such limited words. To the welfare worker I must indeed have looked like a deeply traumatized, virtually feral creature. Although the authorities told Mum that I would have to be enrolled at school, because that was the law, no one could really blame her for trying to keep me away from the rest of the world, taking all the burden of looking after me upon her own shoulders. When they looked at my notes they saw that it was true that I had witnessed my father's death and had been struck dumb as a result, and the picture must have seemed as if it was all clicking neatly into place. The family doctor backed up everything

115

Mum said, confirming that she had taken me to see him soon after Dad's death and that I had already lost the ability to speak by then.

'He's a very aggressive and disturbed child,' he had written, remembering what Mum had told him at the time, and probably remembering our visit all too vividly.

Mum had an explanation for everything.

'Seeing his dad bursting into flames in front of him has tilted his brain,' she explained, using a phrase she had invented herself and would repeat over and over to anyone who'd listen. 'That's why he's so disturbed. He's a terribly fussy eater too. That's why he is as thin as a stick and poorly looking. He's a terrible worry to all of us. It's because he won't eat properly that he has become malnourished and his teeth have all rotted.' She babbled on and on as if the emotional strain of it was more than she could bear, that she had to unburden herself of all her worries now that she had found someone kind enough to listen.

'We know you're a good mother,' the welfare worker gently reassured her, falling completely for the act. 'But you have done wrong by keeping Joe at home and trying to deal with him on your own. We can help you. That's what we're here for. You must trust us to do the best thing for him and for you and the rest of your family.'

Mum seemed to be loving the attention she was getting. Her initial nervousness about how things would go when they found out about me had vanished; she had discovered a way of getting away with everything she and the others had done to me over the previous three years and of coming out looking like a heroine.

Once the welfare worker had gone, having reassured us that everything was going to be fine, Mum stripped me of my new clothes and bundled me straight back downstairs to the cellar. I was quite keen to go before I did something wrong and made her lose her temper. Once I was locked back in the dark I sat on the mattress and thought deeply about everything that had just happened, trying to work out what it all meant.

From my point of view, once I had realized that this woman was actually there to help me rather than kill me, it occurred to me that things could be about to improve dramatically for me. Now the outside world knew that I existed, surely it would become obvious to Mum that she couldn't keep me in the cellar for much longer. If I went to school I would be able to make friends and I wouldn't have to be alone all the time.

Sure enough, a few days later I was taken back upstairs and Mum informed me that things were going to change from now on.

'If you promise me you're going to behave now,' she told me, 'you can move back into Larry and Barry's room.'

Remembering how my older brothers had treated me in the past, I would much rather have gone in with

Thomas and Ellie but I knew that option wasn't on offer so I made no sign or sound of protest. I didn't want to risk upsetting her again by seeming ungrateful for anything she was offering, not when things were just starting to go my way.

'It suits us for you to come out of the cellar now,' Mum told me, 'because Amani wants to use the room for other things.'

I guess she didn't want me to get the idea that she had been made to do anything she didn't want to do just because the welfare worker had been round. She wanted to make it seem as though it was her decision to bring me out of the dark, as if she had decided I had been punished enough now for my past crimes and that I should be allowed to have another chance at living amongst the family to see if I had learned my lesson and mended my ways.

If I thought I was going to get equal treatment to other family members, though, I was sadly mistaken. Even though I was allowed to share my brothers' room, I was still not allowed to play with any of their possessions and I still had none of my own. At teatime on the first night that I was out of the cellar Mum shouted for me to come down from the bedroom, where I had been banished to, to the kitchen. My heart was thumping as I descended the stairs, already able to smell the hot food but not knowing what sort of reception to expect from the others. The rest of the family were all sitting round the table as I stepped hesitantly through the door and I saw there was one empty chair amongst them. I had never sat round the table with them since Dad had died and I felt self-conscious and a bit excited as I lowered myself timidly onto the chair. I was starving and could hardly believe I was actually going to be given proper hot food on a plate. Amani was looking at me strangely so I avoided his gaze, staring hard at the table in front of me, determined not to misbehave or upset anyone and lose my chance of getting fed. I was aware that everyone had gone very quiet, as though they were all waiting for something to happen.

'What the fuck do you think you're doing?' Mum demanded.

I didn't understand what I had done wrong but Amani hit me so hard with the back of his hand that I was sent flying onto the hard tiled floor, back where they all thought I belonged.

'How dare you sit with us, boy?' he snarled down at me. 'What have I told you about behaving yourself, you little bastard?'

'You're putting me off my food,' Mum complained, giving me a sharp kick.

'Get under the table,' Amani commanded, while Larry and Barry sniggered happily. As they threw my food down on the floor, grinding it in with their feet and ordering me to lick up every scrap, I realized nothing had really changed at all.

Now that I was out of the cellar they told me there were new house rules and if I broke them I would be straight back in my cell. My clothes were always to be kept upstairs in the wardrobe and I was only allowed to wear them if I was going to school or if there were visitors to the house. Amani said that I must always put some clothes on if there were other people around because of all my bruises and scars.

'You look disgusting,' he told me. 'A right mess.'

During the times no one had any other use for me I was told I would have to sit in the corner of the bedroom, away from the window, and to do nothing until they had a chore for me. If I was caught playing with anything or disobeying them in any way I would get a taste of Amani's leather belt. I was certainly never allowed to play outside the house. It was as though I had been moved to a different cell, but at least this one was warm and light and smelled better. There were moments when I missed the privacy of my basement. Down there I'd had no idea how slowly time was passing, but in the bedroom I could always see the clock and the hands hardly seemed to move at all as I sat there and stared at it for hours on end, willing them to speed up so another day would be over and I would be closer to the moment when I could escape as Wally had. The sound of the clock would seem to get louder and louder in my head – 'tick tock, tick tock' – as the days ground past. I would put my fingers in my ears to try to shut it out but I never could.

'You can't sleep on the floor any more,' Mum told me. 'You're making the place untidy and you're making the carpet smell. You'll have to share the bed with your brothers.'

Larry and Barry were not pleased to have me in the bed to start with, kicking and punching me all the time to let me know how much they disliked me.

'You stink,' they told me. 'You're an ugly little bastard.'

Amani warned them not to punch me in the face because someone from social services might see the marks, but they were free to do anything else they wanted. It wasn't long before they realized that having me in the bed with them meant they could relieve their sexual frustrations as many times a night as they felt like, just taking turns to rape me, while sometimes using one another for mutual sexual relief as well. They both seemed to like doing it to one another but they always had to force me because it hurt and I didn't like it. If I tried to resist their demands they would tell Mum I was doing something bad and I would get a battering for it. I gave in to almost everything they wanted because anything was better than getting a battering from her, even that. I knew she would never take my side against them and I knew that there was always the threat of being taken back down to the cellar hanging over me. Some nights I was scared of going to sleep because of what I might wake up to find my brothers doing to me, and when I did finally drop off out of exhaustion I would immediately fall into the same nightmares over and over again.

In the dream I would be creeping downstairs, trying to get away from them to the front door. I would be able to see a white light under the door, like a thin slither of freedom on the horizon, but the harder I fought to get to it the more I felt myself being dragged back in slow motion, as if by a terrible weight. If I ever managed to haul myself all the way to the door and pull it open I would immediately wake up in a state of terror. I still sometimes get the same nightmare even today.

My bum was nearly always sore in the morning from the things the boys did to me, and often it was bleeding as well, which made me frightened I would leave a stain on the bedclothes or the carpet, which would have been a punishable offence.

Amani still took me to his bed whenever he felt like discharging his frustrations, even though I was out of the cellar most of the time and everything he did was in plain view of everyone else in the house. He didn't bother to be secretive about it because he didn't care what anyone thought. The whole family knew he did it and they all knew exactly what was going on. Maybe he did it with some of the others as well – I wouldn't know because we never talked about such things. It was as if it was the most normal event in the world for a grown man to be having sex with an eight-year-old boy in his mother's house whenever he wanted to. It was as if I was still there for everyone's convenience and I sort of assumed that was the way life had to be because it had never really been any different since the first time Mum brought me home after Dad's death.

Amani wasn't there every night, I discovered. I found out that he was still staying at Aunt Melissa's as well as at Mum's, moving back and forth between the two of them, getting the best of both worlds. I believe he told Melissa that he was working away from home and it was some time before she found out how complete Mum's revenge against her had been. I don't know how Mum felt about having to share her man with another woman yet again. As it was her doing the stealing of another woman's husband this time, maybe she felt better about it than she had when it was her husband who was messing around.

When I found this out, I hoped briefly that Amani would mention to Melissa some time how badly I was being treated. Surely she would ask what went on at the house? Wouldn't she wonder how I was? But I guess he told her everything was fine, because I never saw or heard from her.

Every night before going to bed Mum had the same routine. She would get Ellie and Thomas up for a wee because otherwise they were likely to wet their mattress, and she began to include me in the ritual too. She would waken us up by shouting at us and dragging us out of bed by our hair at about midnight. She was always drunk by that time of night and the alcohol would have fuelled her anger and resentment towards us, making it impossible for her to resist hitting Thomas and me.

'Get!' she would shout and we would have to scurry to the bathroom to avoid the slaps and kicks she would try to administer along the way.

The effort and inconvenience of it always seemed to stress her out, making the veins stand out on her forehead and her eyes go all bloodshot. It was like having the Incredible Hulk towering over us as we tried to do our business. If Amani was there, he would be waiting for her in bed, which was a disgusting thought in itself, and she would have no patience with us, eager to get back to him. Her breath would stink of alcohol as she pushed her face into ours and bellowed her abuse. I would go first and she could never resist slapping me round the head when I finished and walked past her back to bed. Thomas always had trouble getting the wee to come with her standing over him, screaming at him to hurry up.

'Do you think I'm standing here for my fucking health?' she would yell. 'What's the fucking problem with you?'

I would pull the sheets up over my head to try to block out the sound of my little brother's screams as she whirled him around the bathroom and the landing by his hair, swinging his feet off the ground and then letting go of him, sending him bouncing off the walls. By then I had learned the knack of making myself hit the walls quickly because I knew she found that satisfying. Thomas wasn't as good at it and sometimes just flopped onto the floor, so she would pick him up and do it again and again until she got it right.

One night she was so drunk when she came to get us up she lost her balance and fell over while she was chasing Thomas around, banging her own head on the wall, which pleased me. I could even hear Larry quietly chuckling on the other side of the bed. Seeing his chance, Thomas took it and made a run for his bedroom while she was still down and we all fell silent, knowing that now she would be really mad. She pulled herself unsteadily back to her feet, swearing that this time she truly was going to kill him. I was frightened that she really would so I climbed back out of bed and tried to shield him from her, shaking my head wildly as she bore down on us, as if that would have any effect on her.

'What the fuck are you doing out of bed, you little bastard?' she demanded.

She whacked me around the head and grabbed me by the cheeks, throwing me across the bedroom floor as if I weighed nothing at all. She then lifted Thomas by the throat, dragged him out onto the landing and hurled him down the stairs. I could hear his little body hitting every step on its way to the bottom. I knew exactly how much that hurt from all the times I had been sent tumbling down into the cellar. Then it went eerily quiet for a few seconds before I heard Amani shouting at her angrily.

'What the fuck have you done? It's everywhere.'

'Oh, it's only blood for fuck's sake,' Mum screamed back at him before they disappeared into another room and I couldn't hear what they were talking about any more.

Ten minutes later I heard the sound of an ambulance approaching, siren blaring, and screeching to a stop outside the house. The front door was opened and I strained to listen to what was being said downstairs.

'He lost his balance on the landing,' Mum was telling them in her reasonable voice and they seemed to be accepting her story without any argument.

Mum's sister Pat was staying with us that night and she agreed to go in the ambulance with Thomas. Pat visited from time to time and didn't seem to think there was anything wrong with the way Mum treated us; I suppose that's the way she had been brought up herself by their mother and father. An hour or so after the ambulance took Thomas away the phone rang and I could hear Mum answering it. I could tell from her tone she was talking to Pat.

It sounded to me as though the police hadn't accepted her story quite as easily as the ambulance men had, because she said 'The police are coming round here? Now?' I could hear her telling my aunt what she should tell Thomas to say when they questioned him. I couldn't make out all her words because Barry was snoring.

When he heard the police were on their way Amani left the house fast, pulling on his clothes as he ran out the door. Once he'd gone I heard Mum's footsteps approaching our bedroom. I closed my eyes and pretended to be asleep but she grabbed my hair and pulled me back out of bed.

'Get down to the kitchen,' she ordered me.

I obeyed as quickly as I could, not wanting to be thrown down the stairs as Thomas had been. I could see blood splatters on the steps and across the floor and walls in the hall. Mum followed me into the kitchen and went to a drawer, taking out the biggest, sharpest knife she could find. From the look on her face I felt sure that this time she was going to kill me as she had always promised

127

she would. Her face was contorted with anger as she came towards me. She grabbed hold of me and pressed the blade hard against my throat. I couldn't stop myself from shaking even though I was terrified I would cut myself on the sharp edge if I moved so much as an inch.

'I'm only going to say this once,' she hissed. 'Do you understand?'

I gave a tiny nod.

'The police are coming to the house to ask questions about Thomas falling. I'm going to tell them that you and him got into a fight on the landing and you pushed him down the stairs. Do you understand?'

I nodded again.

'Good boy.'

She took the knife away from my throat and put it back in the drawer. Then she made us both a cup of cocoa as though nothing had happened, as though we did this sort of thing together every night. She gave me a huge fake smile as she handed me the steaming mug to try to calm me down before they arrived and to stop me from shaking.

There was a knock at the door and Mum went to answer it, giving me one more warning. 'Remember what I said.'

I nodded, and sipped cautiously at the hot drink. I could hear a police radio going off in the hallway as she brought them towards the kitchen. I listened to Mum telling her story and she sounded so convincing I was sure they would believe her, as they always did.

'Come into the kitchen and meet him,' she said.

'Hello, young man,' the police officer said as he came in. He was tall and had a loud, deep voice. I glanced up at him and then bowed my head in shame at the lies I was about to have to corroborate. He repeated everything Mum had just told him.

'Is that what happened?' he asked.

'He's a mute,' Mum explained. 'You have to ask him questions that he can nod or shake his head to.'

'Have you been fighting with your little brother, Thomas?' he asked after a moment's thought.

I nodded.

'Did you push him downstairs?'

Nod.

'Well that wasn't very clever, was it?'

Shake.

'I feel sorry for your mum and for poor Thomas. Do you realize that what you did was very serious?'

Nod.

'Are you going to start being a good boy for your mum now?' He gave me a stern look.

I nodded one more time. He shook my hand and said goodbye and I felt so angry inside I thought I was going to explode. If only I could speak. If only I had the ability and the courage to tell him that Mum was lying. She showed him back to the front door, chatting all the way as though she had never done a single thing wrong in her entire life, and I carried on gulping my cocoa until she came back into the kitchen. I wanted to get as much of it inside me as I could before she took it away or threw it all over me.

'Now get back to bed, you little bastard,' she shouted the moment she came into the room and I scurried back upstairs past the bloodstains.

Thomas ended up having twenty or more stitches in his head that night and once more I had been shown to the authorities to be a violent, disruptive child, while Mum came out of it looking like some sort of long-suffering saint.

Almost nobody outside the family ever witnessed the violent side of Mum's personality. She was a Jekyll and Hyde character – all sweetness and light to the authorities and an ogre inside her front door.

There was one exception – our neighbour Paddy. Paddy was from Ireland and drank as much as Mum did. I could never understand a word he was saying but I knew he hated Mum because he would shout at her from outside when the drink had made him brave enough, calling her a 'big fat witch'. Mum had beaten him up several times but he never seemed to learn from his mistakes, his courage bolstered by the Guinness and whisky. One night, soon after I had been released from the cellar, we were all woken up by the sound of him shouting up at the bedroom windows from the street. I could make out Mum's name amongst his slurred, drunken ramblings and I heard her getting out of bed, going downstairs and opening the front door. Larry jumped up and rushed to the bedroom window to see what was happening.

'Go on, Mum,' Larry cheered. 'Holy shit, she's beating him up again.'

I could hear Mum's voice now, drowning out Paddy's shouts. 'You Irish bastard, I'll give you something to knock on my door about in the middle of the fucking night.'

'Come and look at this,' Larry told Barry. 'Hurry up.'

Barry bounced out of bed to take a ringside seat, but I didn't move. I didn't want to watch because I knew what she would be doing and I dreaded to think what was going to happen to poor old Paddy. I also knew that Larry and Barry would have given me a beating if I had tried to join in anyway. I could follow what was going on from listening to their running commentary and from the noises outside as Mum got Paddy round the throat and smashed his head through his own front window, leaving him there to bleed on the jagged edges of the broken glass.

'Shut the window and go back to fucking bed,' she shouted up to the boys before stamping into the house, slamming the door behind her, and going back to bed herself as if nothing had happened. I don't think we heard much more from Paddy after that night. He wasn't exactly the type that could have gone to the police with a coherent story and insisting on pressing charges against her. If he had been, she wouldn't have done it. Mum was too clever to get caught out in the wrong. No matter how much she drank, she always had a survival instinct that allowed her to stay out of trouble herself.

Chapter Nine

Starting School

September rolled round and with it the start of a new school year. The authorities had decided that I was to be put into a normal class with other children my age, but assigned a special teacher to help me. I still couldn't speak beyond making a few primitive and unintelligible sounds and I certainly couldn't read or write. I was eight years old and all the other kids in the classes had been in school for three or four years by then and had developed mentally way beyond anywhere I could have got to sitting alone in my cell in the dark.

I knew a bit of what to expect at school from the stories that Wally had told me, but it was hardly enough to prepare me for the full-scale assault on my senses from every direction when I first went back out into the hustle and bustle of the real world. I had spent three years virtually on my own, in a world that was largely silent and dark, and now I was out in the dazzling light of day, surrounded by crowds of kids all rushing around and jostling one another and laughing, with bells going off and teachers shouting out orders and books being thrown around. There were so many strange faces and so many new rules to learn in order to fit in and become part of it all. I must have looked like an odd, nervous little creature as I stepped through the school gates for the first time, with little idea what to expect. The kids all crowded up to me, curious to find out about the strange new boy in their midst.

'Hi,' they said, their faces all around me, staring, weighing me up, trying to judge me and work out whether I was going to make any difference to their lives. 'What's your name?'

'He don't speak,' my brothers told them.

'What do you mean, he don't speak?' They stepped back, regarding me with a mixture of curiosity and suspicion. Kids don't like anyone different or strange. I could see it wasn't going to be easy for me to make any friends.

Each school morning the routine I had to follow was the same. My clothes would be neatly laid out for me at the bottom of the bed and I would try to get dressed quickly so I didn't drip blood anywhere from where Larry and Barry had penetrated me in the night. Once I was dressed I had to sit back in the corner of the room, 'the dirty corner' as they all called it, and wait until they told me what to do next.

Mum would call me down when she was ready and I would be allowed two pieces of plain buttered bread and a drink of water. The bread was served to me in my dog bowl and the water in a plastic beaker with my name on it because I still wasn't allowed to contaminate any of the other crockery that the rest of the family used. I didn't mind too much because at least it was regular food and I didn't feel so starved all the time as I had in the cellar. Larry and Barry would escort me to school, a chore they obviously resented enormously. I would walk five or six paces behind with my head down, staring at the pavement, lost in thoughts about Dad, unable to get him out of my mind. I would count the paving stones as I went to try to distract myself from the sound of his voice inside my head.

'Hurry up, Joe,' they would grumble bossily. 'Stop dawdling. We'll tell Mum if you don't get a fucking move on.'

Thomas and I weren't allowed to do PE at school because then we would have had to get undressed in front of other people, so Mum would send in sick notes asking for us to be exempted. With me she claimed it was because of my asthma, with Thomas it was because of his 'hole in the heart'. Apparently he had had a hole when he was born, but it had closed up pretty quickly and never gave him any problems. She told the school it would be dangerous for him to do any physical exercise and the teachers chose to believe her. I was quite relieved she did that because I wouldn't have wanted other boys asking questions about our scars and bruises. It didn't occur to me that if the staff saw them it might alert someone to our plight, which might lead to us being rescued. No one had ever made any attempt to rescue us before and I knew Mum would always have a story ready to explain any marks that might have raised suspicions.

'Oh, the boys are always fighting and hitting each other,' she'd say if challenged. Or, 'He fell downstairs because he was messing about, as usual.'

The other thing that worried me was that if other boys had asked us what really happened Thomas would have come right out with the reason for the marks because he was always more confident than me. I was already being teased enough without my new classmates finding out my whole family used me as a punch bag.

Even once I was at school every day, things still didn't go smoothly at home with Mum. Once we were behind closed doors and drawn curtains she continued to rule the family in the same violent way she always had. It didn't matter if I was going to school because I wasn't able to talk and tell anyone any tales. Even if I had been able to I doubt she would have worried. She was always confident that she had intimidated me just as completely as she had intimidated the others. None of us would ever have dared to betray her for fear of the consequences and for fear of being told we were liars. We truly believed she was capable of killing us if we pushed her too far. If I annoyed her too much she would just make excuses to the school and keep me off, telling them I was ill, and would banish me back down to the cellar until her mood had brightened again.

Soon after the beginning of term she left me alone down there in my old cell for three whole days after I did something that offended her, without allowing anyone to come and see me or to bring me down any scraps. I knew how long it was because I watched the daylight coming and going three times through the holes in the airbrick. By the second day the hunger pains were unbearable and I curled myself up into a ball to try to squeeze them away, rocking back and forth and telling myself to imagine I had just eaten an apple, trying to fool my stomach into believing it was full. I had finished the bottle of water she had left me with by the second night and I think I must have been passing in and out of consciousness by then. I tried eating little bits of plastic from the bottle to ease the hunger pains, but it just made them worse.

On the third day Mum went off to visit her mother. I heard her footsteps going down the path outside the airbrick but I didn't actually have the strength to lift my head in order to watch her shadow pass. A while later I heard someone coming down the stairs and unlocking the door.

'Here, boy,' Amani said. He always called me boy, never actually using my name. 'I've made you a cup of tea and some toast.'

I didn't believe he was being genuine for a second. I was certain he was playing some new sort of mind game with me. He had probably put something on the toast that would make me sick, or had spat into the tea or worse. But at the same time I was so hungry I didn't want to pass up the chance of food even if there was going to be some sort of horrible price to pay for it. I lay still, not able to find the strength to sit up. I could smell the warm toast and it made my saliva glands work, making my jaw ache painfully with anticipation. Amani crouched down beside me, tore a piece of crust off one of the slices and held it against my lips. I was frightened that it might be poisoned but I still couldn't resist parting my lips and letting him push the toast in. He was acting so out of character I didn't know what to expect next.

'Honestly, boy,' he said gently. 'It's okay, you can eat it. It'll make you feel better.'

I closed my eyes and opened my mouth for more, expecting to receive a punch or a stamp on the head as I chewed, but nothing happened and the toast tasted good. After a few moments I opened my eyes and saw that he was just sitting watching me, waiting for me to sit up and take a sip of the tea he had brought me.

'You look great, boy,' he said. 'I'm sorry I've been acting so bad to you. It's your mother you know. She tells me to do these things. She brings out the worst in me.'

I flinched as he rubbed the top of my head with the palm of his giant hand and gave a forced smile. I could believe that he thought he was telling the truth, but I didn't think Mum had to work too hard to get him to do any of the things he did to me. I wanted to win him over by showing how humble I was in his presence, as if he was a god or something, but I'm sure my eyes must still have shown how frightened I felt. He went on trying to reassure me, trying to be friendly. He told me to come upstairs with him and helped me up the steps and into the house. He took me into Mum's good lounge, sitting me down on the settee even though I was still dirty from the floor of the cellar. I perched right on the edge of the cushions, frightened I might leave a mark that she would see and punish me for when she came back.

'I'll cook you something nice later,' Amani was saying. 'Be careful not to spill that tea on your mother's furniture.'

The phone went and I could tell from his tone when he picked it up that he was speaking to Mum. 'No, love,' he reassured her. 'He's alive and well. I gave him some toast and tea and he looks good as new.'

Had she believed that she might finally have killed me? Was that why she'd gone out and sent Amani down to check up on me?

'When's he coming?' Amani was asking. 'Fifteen minutes? Okay … No, I'm sure he's going to be a good boy now.'

He was looking back at me as he spoke, as if he was issuing a warning, and I was even more sure that he was being nice to me for a reason, that he had something planned for me.

'Come with me,' he said once he'd hung up the phone and we headed upstairs to the bedroom, my heart sinking at the thought of what he might do to me now. I stayed a few paces behind in case he turned and kicked me back down the stairs, but he was still making out he wanted to be nice to me, as if we were allies in some way. In the bedroom he took out some of my school uniform and told me to put it on. I didn't understand why because I wasn't going to school that day, but I obeyed him anyway. Once I was dressed he took me through to Mum's room.

'Sit on the bed,' he instructed and I obeyed, terrified that she would come back unexpectedly and catch me in there, but too frightened of him to disobey for even a second.

Just then I heard someone knocking at the front door.

'Stay there,' he told me. 'Don't make a sound.'

140

I heard another man's voice downstairs as Amani let him in. It sounded creepy as they mumbled and laughed together, obviously not wanting me to overhear what they were saying, as if they had some dodgy deal going. I sat waiting on the end of the bed. I heard footsteps on the stairs and the door opened. A stumpy-looking man with a fat stomach and thinning hair came in. His t-shirt was too short for him and his belly hung out beneath it over his belt. He was carrying a big black bag.

'Hello, mate,' he said. 'My name is Douglas. I'm your friend. You can call me Uncle Douglas.'

I tried to look round him for Amani but I couldn't see any sign of him.

'Would you like a sweet?' Douglas asked, pushing the door shut behind him. I nodded cautiously and he put some sort of jellybean into my hand, which I chewed and swallowed quickly in case he took it off me again. It tasted good, setting my saliva glands watering again.

'Wow,' he laughed at my eagerness. 'You liked that, didn't you?'

He gave me another one. I couldn't understand why he was being so nice to me but I wasn't going to pass up the chance of free sweets. He didn't seem to be at all aggressive and I was starting to feel a little more at ease.

'You don't have to worry,' he said. 'I'm here to help you.'

Amani poked his head round the door at that moment and I wondered if he had heard and was going to beat the man up. 'Everything okay?' he asked.

'Yes, of course,' Douglas replied. 'He's a nice lad.'

'Okay then,' Amani grinned, showing all his huge teeth. 'I'll leave you two alone to get to know each other better.'

So many different thoughts were going round in my head I couldn't make any sense of them, or of what was going on. I sensed danger but couldn't see exactly where it was coming from. Mum could be nice like this some-times, and then turn nasty again in a split second. Would Uncle Douglas be like that if I said the wrong thing or looked at him in the wrong way?

'Wow, you are such a fine boy,' Douglas was saying and his words made me feel proud. I wasn't used to compliments. 'Shall we play a fun game?'

It had been a long time since I'd had someone take so much interest in me or be that nice. No one had ever suggested playing a game with me since the day Dad died. In fact they had pretty much forbidden me from even thinking of doing such a thing. Douglas was sitting on the bed too and started to tickle me. Then he gave me another sweet. He smelled bad when he got close, a mixture of stale sweat, bad breath and unwashed clothes,

142

but I was used to unpleasant smells. I can't have smelled that fresh myself after three days in the cellar. Reaching into his bag he took out a camera.

'Can I take some pictures of you to show to my wife?' he asked. 'Is that okay with you?'

I nodded and he gave me another sweet. I rather liked the idea of someone taking my picture. Dad used to do it when he was alive, because he was proud of me and wanted to show my picture off to other people.

'Lie on the bed then,' he said.

I did what he told me, wondering if perhaps he was going to adopt me and that was why he had to show a picture to his wife. I liked that idea. Anything to get away from Mum.

'It's hot in here, why don't you take off your jumper?' He helped me pull it over my head and undid a few of my shirt buttons for me. 'That's better,' he said, giving me another sweet.

'Let's see if you can take your shirt and trousers off by the time I count to ten,' he said next. 'If you can, I'll give you some more sweets.'

I had spent so many years just in my pants that I thought nothing of it. The sweets, on top of the toast and tea, were making me feel quite good. He told me to bounce on the bed for some more pictures and I did as he suggested, feeling exhilarated. I hadn't had so much fun for years.

'Just take your pants off,' he said casually, 'and lie back down on the bed.'

It was as if someone had just switched off all the fun and every alarm bell in my brain was ringing at once. I sat very still and shook my head. This was the sort of thing Mum and Amani and Larry and Barry would make me do. I wanted to go on having fun. I didn't want to be hurt.

'Don't be shy,' he laughed as he saw me hesitate, as if I was just being silly. 'It's just for fun.'

I gave another shake of my head.

'Don't be naughty,' he warned and there was a slight edge of menace in his voice, which made me shiver and want to cry. 'Be a good boy, otherwise I'll have to call your daddy.'

I gave another shake of the head and suddenly a slap landed on my face so hard that it knocked me sideways. He raised his hand to strike again but I had already jumped up and sunk my teeth into the side of his palm. I dug them in deeper and deeper, just as I had with the welfare worker. I was able to taste the blood, keeping my jaw locked, frightened of what would happen once I let go. Douglas gave a shout of pain and Amani came running in and punched me so hard on the side of my head that my jaw sprang open and Douglas was able to leap back, flapping his hand around in the air. Amani flew into the most terrible rage I had ever seen him in and ripped his belt out of its loops, hitting me over and over again with it while Douglas held me down on the bed to stop me from trying to escape. Douglas then sat on my head, forcing my face into the mattress. I couldn't move or protect myself as both of them raped me in turn. It was the first time I had been abused by anyone outside the family. They did disgusting things to me that I had never had done before, things that hurt me very badly, and they took photographs of one another with Douglas's camera as they did them.

When they had finally finished with me, Amani dragged me downstairs by the hair, all the way to the cellar, just as Mum would have done. I lost my footing several times on the stairs but he never lost his grip.

'Just can't do what you are fucking told, can you, boy?' he screamed. 'You'll learn one of these days.'

With one final kick he propelled me into the cell, leaving me naked and bleeding on the concrete floor. As my strength returned over the following hours I managed to crawl onto the mattress and a terrible rage grew inside me, fed by the hunger that the toast and sweets had only temporarily subdued. I tried to scream in order to get the anger out, but my throat still wouldn't allow it. It was as if everything was locked inside my head and I was afraid I was falling apart. I eventually pulled myself to my feet and started kicking the door with my heels, louder and louder, like a mad caged animal. My heart was pounding and then Amani exploded back through the door. He had a cigar clenched between his teeth.

'You little bastard! You think you're clever, don't you?'

I lashed out at him with my fists, punching his belly as hard as I could, but he just stood there and laughed at my puny efforts. Eventually tiring of the sport he grabbed my throat and lifted me up. I could feel the heat of his cigar on my face and I thought he was going to burn my eyes out. He blew a cloud of smoke at me and the cigar fell on the floor.

'Now look what you've made me do!'

I could hardly breathe and I was certain I was going to die when he threw me across the room as if I weighed nothing. My back slammed against the wall, knocking the wind out of me. I fell onto the mattress, gasping for breath and watched as he walked across the cell towards me, unzipping his trousers. He pulled out his willy and before I could duck out of the way, he peed all over my face.

'Thirsty, are you?' he laughed as I struggled to breathe without letting any of it get into my mouth. 'Why didn't you just ask for a drink?'

When he'd finished he made a gargling noise in his throat and then spat into my face before walking to the door.

'If you need anything else,' he said, 'just ring,' and he laughed, very pleased with his own joke.

Picking his cigar up off the floor he clamped it back into his mouth and left, locking the door behind him and turning out the light. I lay in the dark trying to take in what had just happened to me and to work out what it might mean for the future.

Chapter Ten

Being Groomed

After the introduction to Uncle Douglas, Amani brought several more men down to my cell to have sex with me. They usually came at weekends or during school holidays, but sometimes I was kept off school on a weekday and taken down to the cellar and I would know exactly what was in store for me.

It was as though after the experience with Uncle Douglas I had passed some sort of test and shown myself to be ready for the market. They were all strong and I soon gave up trying to resist them or fight them off. It was pointless because I was an undernourished nine-year-old and they were all grown men. Every protest I made just earned me a beating each time, which merely delayed the inevitable and meant that I would eventually be left in more pain than I would have to endure if I simply gave in and co-operated. It was better to let them get on with whatever it was they wanted to do to me so it would be over as quickly as possible and they would go away and leave me alone sooner. Amani kept telling me that everything that happened in my cell or inside the house had to remain a closely guarded secret. He pretended that it was for my own good that no one else found out.

'If anyone ever finds out about this,' he told me, 'they will go to the police and they will put you in jail.'

I believed him because one of the men who came to the cell had told me he was a policeman and I had never had any reason to doubt the truth of that statement. The visiting policeman made sure I knew that he had locked up lots of little boys like me in the past, and he was always using his steel handcuffs on me in the cell. They seemed to be part of the thrill for him.

'If you ever go to any of my friends at the police station and tell them what goes on here,' he warned me, 'I will get to hear about it and then I'll come back here and kill you. Do you understand?'

I would always nod and keep my eyes averted, never wanting to look as though I was challenging them or being insolent. I had no cause to doubt that all these men would be willing to kill me if they felt they had to in order to protect themselves. Maybe they would even enjoy doing it. But it never occurred to me to tell anyone else anyway. Their secrets were safe with me. After all the things that had happened to me in the previous few years I had no reason to think that anyone would believe me or help me or make my life more bearable in any way. If even policemen were doing this sort of thing to children, who was there left for me to turn to? Since I still couldn't speak or write I couldn't imagine how they thought I was going to tell anyone anything. My situation was completely hopeless. I was entirely cut off from the rest of the world in my silence.

I suppose it was at this stage that Mum realized she could earn some money from the services I was being forced to provide to Amani's friends. She started gloating to me during my beatings that she was going to make money off me, and lots of it, but at the time I couldn't understand what she meant. I thought perhaps it was something to do with the nuts and the cuckoo that Wally had told me were in her head; maybe they were making her imagine stuff. How could a little boy like me make her lots of money, particularly if I never left the house apart from going to school? It gradually dawned on me that the visitors to the house, such as Uncle Douglas, must be paying her for the privilege of doing things to me. Since I had always been made to do these sorts of things with family members for free anyway I wondered if this might turn out to be a good thing, despite the fact that it hurt and I hated doing it. Perhaps Mummy would love me more if I managed to earn her some money? If

I was very successful at it, I reasoned, maybe she would even let me have regular food and a warm room, wanting to keep me fit and healthy so I could keep on working for her for longer.

'Uncle Douglas is going to be taking you for a day out,' she told me a couple of weeks after I first met him. She then shouted at me a lot, wanting to be sure I understood how badly she would hurt me if I didn't do exactly as I was told when I was with him.

'You won't be hurt any more if you do what Mummy says,' Amani told me when he came to my cell to get me on the day of the planned outing. I nodded to show I understood, carefully avoiding looking up at him. 'But if this ever gets out,' he went on, 'I'll cut your fucking eyes out. Come with me.'

I obediently followed him upstairs to the bathroom with no idea what lay in store for me. He ordered me into the shower and scrubbed me down roughly in the water. I suppose he wanted to get rid of all the smells on my flesh, including the recent stink of his own urine.

'Are you ready for this, boy?' he laughed. 'You're up for sale.'

I remembered Wally telling me that no one else should be allowed to touch my private parts. He was the only person I'd ever met who seemed to believe that so I supposed he must have been mistaken. He wasn't like any of the others in the family so maybe he was the strange one, not them. He had gone now anyway, so maybe Amani and Mum and Larry and Barry and Uncle Douglas were all right and I just had to put up with whatever they wanted to do to me. Everything in my life hurt, both physically and mentally, and the years I had spent coping with it had left me numb, as well as angry and miserable. I was tired of even thinking about it because it never made any difference.

When Uncle Douglas came to collect me that day money openly changed hands in the hallway, but I don't know how much because I didn't dare to look up from the floor. If Mum caught me looking at transactions like that I would get a real beating. Uncle Douglas was as charming with Mum as she was with him; anyone would have thought it was her he had called for as they flirted away with one another. While he waited in the passage-way she hauled me into the kitchen for what she called 'a prep talk'.

'Right, you no good little bastard,' she hissed. 'Make sure you do whatever Uncle Douglas says. He's my best customer and if I find out you haven't done what he tells you I will fucking kill you when you get back.'

She grabbed me by the throat and stared into my eyes.

'Do we understand each other?'

I nodded and she transferred her iron grip to my wrist, leading me back out to where Douglas was waiting. He gripped my wrist even harder than her, frightened, I suppose, that I would do a runner the moment I was outside the front door.

'What time do you want him home?' he asked her.

'About eightish?' she suggested. 'Enjoy yourselves. Be good, Joe.'

Anyone overhearing them would have thought she was seeing me off for an afternoon at the zoo with my favourite uncle. Douglas smiled down at me as he led me out to his dark blue Ford car, opening the back door so I could climb in, as if he really was my uncle and we really were going for a nice day out together.

'That's a good boy,' he said cheerily. 'In you get. Put your belt on.'

The moment he slammed the door and walked round to the driver's side I panicked and tried to make a bid for freedom. I wrenched at the handle, intending to make a run for it. I don't know where I thought I could have run to; I just knew I didn't want to go with him. A horrible feeling of dread gripped my stomach as the handle moved but the door stayed firmly locked. It was like being in a nightmare where I had no control over my surroundings or anything that was happening to me. He must have been able to hear exactly what I was trying to do, but he stayed calm as he climbed into his seat, looking back over his shoulder at me and smiling again. He knew full well there was no way I could get out of that car; as we set off I noticed that the winding mechanisms for the rear windows had been removed. It was as though I was travelling as a prisoner in the back of a police van, being transported between jail cells.

Once I realized there was no way of escaping I didn't want to make a fuss and risk getting a beating from him, or from Mum when I got home, so I stayed still and waited to see what would happen next. I knew from experience that if I gave him any cheeky looks or struggled at all I would get punched.

I noticed he had a bible in the front with him. In the coming months I discovered he always seemed to have one around him somewhere. It's hard to understand how he could reconcile the things he read in those pages with the things he did in his own life, but he never seemed to be a man who was troubled by his conscience. Maybe he had managed to convince himself that he was doing God's work in some way. Whenever he was waiting for someone and had a few minutes to spare he would open the good book and read a few pages. He was often mumbling to himself in those quiet moments, like some old nutter in the park. Maybe he hoped he was securing himself a place in Heaven. Some hope.

The journey lasted about an hour and Douglas talked most of the way, his voice pleasant one moment and aggressive the next, telling me all the things he liked to do to little boys like me, and to little girls as well. I didn't want to listen to him but I wasn't particularly shocked by anything he said because I'd heard Amani and Larry and Barry talking in the same way many times, as well as the other visitors Amani had brought to my cell. I thought I knew pretty much all the things that people like Uncle Douglas liked to do to children.

When we got close to our destination he pulled the car into a secluded lay-by and started shouting at me, just as Mum had, telling me over and over again that if I made a noise or acted up he would kill me. He produced a knife from the glove compartment and waved it in the air. Knowing how violent he had been at the house I didn't doubt that he would be willing to use it. He was just as frightening as Mum and Amani. Once he thought he had intimidated me enough he drove off again and a few minutes later he turned into the car park of a rural hotel. He tucked the car round a corner out of sight of the building. He switched off the engine, turned round and gave me a final warning not to cross him, then he showed me a gun he had in his pocket. I'm not sure if it was real or just a toy one, but it was enough to terrify me anyway. I was even more scared of that gun than I was of the knife in the glove compartment.

'If you try to run,' he told me, 'I will shoot you and cut your body up into tiny pieces.'

I was so frightened I nearly wet myself.

He climbed out and slammed the door behind him. He went to the back of the car, opened the boot and then opened the door nearest to me. He pulled me out of my seat and round to the back, lifted me up and dropped me into the open boot as if I was an old suitcase.

'Stay calm and keep quiet,' he ordered. 'If you make a sound I will kill you.'

He slammed the lid shut, leaving me shivering in the dark, listening to his disappearing footsteps. I wondered how much air there was; was I going to suffocate before he got back? What if something happened to him and no one knew I was there? How long would it be before someone found my body? I felt as though I was already lying in my coffin.

Uncle Douglas must have gone into the hotel to check in and get a key. A few minutes later I heard a woman's voice outside. For a split second I considered shouting out for help and banging on the roof, but then I thought better of it, remembering how convincing he had been when he talked about killing me, and realizing that this woman might be a friend of his, just like Mum. The voices faded away again. A few minutes later there were more footsteps.

'It's only me,' Uncle Douglas whispered. 'Everything's going to be okay.'

He opened the boot and helped me out. I was shaking but he was obviously nervous too, darting furtive looks around him all the time. 'Be a good boy and you won't get hurt,' he said. 'You know the rules.'

He had a gold key in his hand attached to a large number on a plastic key ring. He hurried me through some bushes to the door of a chalet-style hotel room slightly separated from the rest of the hotel. He held onto me with one hand as he used the key to open the door with the other. Inside was a large double bedroom. He shut and locked the door behind us. He pulled the curtains and immediately led me through into the ensuite bathroom. Then he told me to undress and get into the shower with him.

Once we were both standing under the water he touched my private parts, telling me how nice it all was and then suddenly lifted me up by the armpits so that my face was level with his. It was as if he had suddenly gone into a frenzy. He was kissing, licking and biting me, sinking his vile yellow old teeth into my chest and neck. His breath stank so badly it made me want to be sick. The assault seemed to go on forever and when he finally let me go and I dropped in a heap at his feet I thought he must have finished, but he hadn't. Grabbing my hair and pulling it till I whimpered with the pain, he forced my face onto his private parts and continued to live out his fantasy, calling me a dirty little pig and a stream of other names. He ordered me to swallow his semen or he would beat me and I knew I had no choice, almost choking as I tried to get it down.

When he had eventually finished he gave me a hard slap round the head.

'You're a good boy,' he said. 'Show me how much you've enjoyed yourself. Go on, smile. Lick your lips.'

I did as I was told, trying to look happy and to hold back the tears, then he went back to insulting me and telling me I was filthy and how I loved his cock. It was as if he was angry with me for what had happened, as if it showed I was a filthy piece of dirt because I wanted to do stuff like that. Then he seemed to decide he wanted a break.

'Stay in here until I'm ready for you again,' he ordered and went through into the bedroom, leaving me lying in a heap in the corner of the shower, my chest heaving with sobs, the water still pouring down over me as I curled up into a ball, my arms wrapped around my legs. About fifteen minutes must have passed before he came back in, still naked, sipping a cup of tea he'd made himself. To my horror I saw that he was stiff again as he told me what game he wanted to play next.

'You've got to learn how to play these games,' he told me, placing his teacup carefully down on a shelf. 'If you make any mistakes next time I will be causing you severe pain.'

He was playing with himself again, apparently taking pleasure in watching me crying and seeing the fear in my eyes. As he dragged me by the hair into the bedroom I clung onto his wrists, trying to lessen the pain. He hurled me onto the bed, ordering me to lie on my stomach before tying my wrists and ankles to the bed frames and smacking me really violently with his hands. The more I struggled the more he enjoyed it, pleasuring himself over and over again and then eventually lying down on top of me, almost suffocating me in his layers of smelly, sweaty, flabby flesh, squeezing my neck hard, forcing my body to allow him to penetrate me.

'What a good boy you are,' he would tell me every time he finished, but then he would start on some new, violent humiliation.

When he eventually needed a rest he tied me to the radiator in the bathroom and went off, locking the doors behind him, telling me not to make a sound till he got back. I was left squatting naked on the cold tiles, feeling sick with disgust at everything that had been done to me, as well as terrified about what was still to come. My head was spinning and every part of me was in agony. I didn't think I could survive any more pain.

When Uncle Douglas returned an hour or so later his breath smelled of drink so I imagine he must have been sitting in the hotel bar, gloating over his sexual adventures. He was carrying a glass of water and bent down to lift my floppy head so that I could take some sips from it. He untied me and told me to take another shower but as I stood up I fainted. I was probably only unconscious for a few minutes and when I came round he had lifted me into the shower and was washing me again. He then dried me off and carried me through to the bedroom and dressed me as if nothing had happened. He carried me out to the car and chucked my lifeless body onto the back seat, leaving the key inside the hotel room for the staff to find.

When I got home I was carried back down to the basement and left on my mattress to recover. Although I didn't understand it at the time, my grooming had begun in earnest.

Chapter Eleven

The Movie Business

Initially I was a bit of a novelty for the other kids at school – the first mute boy any of them had ever met – but it wasn't long before that novelty had worn off and I was just another easy target for teasing and bullying. I was used to being a victim; it was a part I had been playing for years and nothing any of the other kids said or did to me came close to the horrors that I had already experienced at home or with Uncle Douglas, but it still made me sad to feel excluded from everyone around me yet again. I would have loved to make some friends but no one wanted to hang out with me because I was different and weird. A lot of them found it impossible to resist teasing me, knowing I couldn't answer back. What was so wrong with me, I wondered, that everyone seemed to want to have a go at me all the time? Maybe I had inherited Dad's genes and was just as horrible and wicked as

Mum had always told me I was. Maybe it was all Dad's fault that my life was the way it was, as Wally had said – but deep down I knew that Dad was still the only person who had ever really loved me.

The girls at school were even worse than the boys when it came to picking on someone who couldn't answer back. They danced round me all the time, taunting me, calling me 'Dumbty Dumbty'.

'Do you want a sweetie?' they'd ask, all fake smiles and fluttering eyes. 'Was that a "no"? Or a "yes"? Must have been a "no" I guess!' And then they would run off laughing, leaving me still struggling to get the right word out. I could think of so many things I wanted to say but they had to remain bottled up inside me, simmering up to the boil.

The worst time was lunchtime because I couldn't sneak off and find a quiet corner somewhere. I had to go into the canteen with everyone else if I wanted to eat, and I was always starving. The dinner ladies were kind and did their best to protect me at times when there weren't any teachers around, going mad at my tormentors when they caught them and sending them off to the headmaster. But the bullies just got more sly, digging me painfully in the ribs when the grown-ups were looking away or pinching me under the table, safe in the knowledge that I wouldn't make a sound. I was an outcast, just a dummy and a punch bag. Thomas used to stick up for me whenever he was nearby, even though he was three years younger than me. He'd kick anyone he caught picking on me with all his growing strength, but he had friends of his own age and didn't want to be standing guard over me every hour of the day.

'Don't talk to my brother like that!' he'd shout whenever he caught them in the act, and they would all take notice of him, however old they were.

Thomas was turning into a hard little nut, happy to give anyone a kicking if they tried it on with him. I didn't fight back myself because I'd learned how much worse things got for me at home when I did that. Teachers were still using canes and slippers to beat children in school back then and I didn't want to risk that. In fact, I did end up getting beaten once or twice for being disruptive in class and it wasn't as dreadful as I had feared. I was so hardened to punishment I didn't even react when they swiped me across the knuckles with a cane. Pain didn't have much effect on me by then; I used to inflict it on myself anyway. Sometimes I would scrape pen nibs along my arm, digging them into the flesh from the sheer frustration of being me and having to live the life I had been given and being so helpless to do anything about making it better. There were times when I felt as though I hated me as much as Mum and the others did, and I thought I could understand why they always wanted to hit me.

165

There was one boy in my year called Pete who never joined in any of the attacks on me and started coming to my rescue whenever he saw I was being bullied. He came from a more educated family than most of us; his father was a doctor and his mother was a university lecturer. He knew that what they were doing was out of order and he started sticking up for me, apparently not afraid of anyone. He and Thomas were the only ones who had ever done that. Wally had been kind to me, but he had tried to avoid taking a beating himself on my behalf, and had never confronted the others and told them that what they were doing to me was wrong. Pete knew what was right and what was wrong and he wasn't willing to keep quiet about it. You don't meet many people who are brave enough to be like that, particularly not children, and I felt proud when I realized that such a good and brave person wanted to be my friend.

Pete was pretty tough physically so he doled out the odd clip round the ear on my behalf when my attackers wouldn't back down and he started to get into trouble for it with the staff. His parents were called into the school to talk about his behaviour, which the staff all thought was out of character. All his mum and dad knew was that their previously bright and well-behaved son had only started to get into trouble since befriending me, the strange, grubby, skinny little mute boy, so they obviously jumped to the conclusion that I was a bad influence on him. In fact all Pete was doing was watching my back and being protective. He was my Good Samaritan and I wished I could find the words to tell them that they should be proud of his behaviour, not worried about it.

I used to get my head shoved down the toilets a lot by the bigger boys, so Pete would make sure he accompanied me every time I needed to go. The bullies wouldn't do anything if he was there to challenge them and make them feel like cowards. He'd been quite popular before but the other children tried to isolate him because I was always with him and they didn't want me, 'the freak', hanging around with them. But Pete never let me down. If he had to choose between me and his former friends then he always chose me, and they were forced to respect that once they realized they couldn't turn him against me. Watching the way he dealt with them was a lesson to me and I wished I could stand up to everyone in my life the way he stood up to those kids.

I'd started speech therapy lessons with a woman called Jill, but progress was very slow in the beginning. Pete never got impatient with me when I couldn't communicate with him verbally. I would point to something, or draw a picture, or make an expression and he would always understand what I was on about. He worked hard at it but never made it seem like a chore. He was an only child, which was maybe why he was less willing to hunt with the pack and was not frightened of standing up for what he thought was right, even if it meant being ostracized himself.

'I'd love you to be my brother,' he told me several times. 'I'd look after you all the time then.'

Can you imagine what it felt like to have someone say things like that to me when I had spent the last three years being told what a filthy, smelly, evil little bastard I was?

Despite the misgivings Pete's parents had about their son's unusual choice of friend, they invited me back to their home after school one day. They lived in a big smart house and I felt incredibly nervous, imagining what sort of reception I would get. I was shaking as we crunched across the gravel towards the imposing-looking front door, knowing exactly how Mum always reacted to any children who made unwelcome visits to our house. Pete was hoping that if his parents actually met me and got to know me they wouldn't be so worried about me hanging out with him because they would see that I was a nice guy. Personally, I was very doubtful that I was going to be able to impress them when I didn't even have the power of speech, but I was anxious to try – and curious also to see what life was like in a family so different from mine.

I had never been to anyone else's home apart from other family members when Dad was alive, and I had certainly never been inside such a lovely house with posh cars parked on the drive and expensive furniture in every room. There was a real feeling of warmth and love and security the moment you walked through the door, a million miles from the cheap, neat, show-home look that Mum struggled to maintain in her best lounge. Pete's father was a tall man with a deep, commanding voice. He and his mother were incredibly welcoming and tried to make polite conversation with me as we had tea sitting at their huge oak kitchen table. Pete did the talking for me, translating my noises and gestures and expressions. It seemed to me that they were way above me in every sense, that I didn't deserve to be sitting with them and should probably be under the table as I would have been at home. To be treated with such kindness and respect was an overwhelming experience but at the same time it gave me hope because it made me realize that there was a world where people were gentle and polite and protective towards one another. Maybe one day, I thought, I would be able to escape from my background and live a life more like this.

Not having the slightest understanding of what life might be like in a home like mine, Pete innocently came knocking at Mum's front door one day to ask if I could come out to play.

'Fuck off!' Mum told him the moment he opened his mouth to speak. 'Don't come knocking my door again.'

She slammed the door in his startled face and I suspect in that moment he suddenly understood a great deal more about me and why I was the way I was, even without knowing the gruesome details. Her reaction wasn't personal to him; she talked the same way to any kids who came round for us, so they only ever tried once. She didn't want to have other kids hanging around the house, asking questions, seeing things that they shouldn't and telling tales back at their own homes. She didn't make any attempt to turn on the false charm for them; it was only the adults in positions of authority who she was polite to, putting on her big act when she thought she was about to get into trouble or when she wanted to scrounge some more benefit money.

I was over the moon at having a real friend of my own and looked forward to getting to school each day just to see him. Another advantage of school for me was that I knew I would get at least one meal a day, five days a week, and I made the most of it. I would eat twice as fast as everyone else and keep on going back up for third, fourth and sometimes even fifth helpings, pointing at the food and looking at the dinner ladies with imploring eyes. I ate like a pig, clearing my plate and anyone else's that was within reach. It became a standing joke amongst the dinner ladies and they loved it. It was a compliment to their cooking I guess.

'You need fattening up,' they would laugh as they heaped more and more food onto my plate. 'You can have as much as you want, love.'

My favourite was the apple crumble with loads of custard. It filled my stomach with a satisfying weight that I could feel lying inside me for several hours afterwards, a completely different feeling to the endless hours of hunger pains that I had grown used to in Mum's house. It wasn't long before I started to put on weight and regain some of the strength and health that had ebbed away over the previous years of starvation and imprisonment. It's amazing how a young body can recover from so much abuse and actually catch up on the growing that it's missed once you start to nourish it a bit.

There were several more weekend trips to the hotel in the country with Uncle Douglas, and the routine was always the same. Mum would be paid in advance and warned that if I didn't do it right she wouldn't be paid again next time, so she made it clear to me each time what she would do to me if I didn't please her best customer. He would then go through pretty much the same rituals every time, torturing and raping and humiliating me for hours on end, making sure that he could rely on my absolute co-operation and obedience with threats and beatings. Although he was pleasing himself and living out his own fantasies, Douglas was also preparing me for something else, breaking me in so that he could be sure he could sell my services to others and be confident that I would never let him down or cause any trouble. I was being trained just like an animal in the circus.

'You're going to be making big films,' Mum said one day when she was yet again getting me ready to be picked up from the house by Uncle Douglas. 'You'll be becoming an actor.'

Her words puzzled me. How could that be possible, I wondered, when I couldn't speak or even make a sound?

'You've got to prove you're worthwhile otherwise I won't be paid,' she reminded me. 'You're going to be the youngest porn star ever.'

I wasn't sure what a porn star was. Porn was a type of fish wasn't it? Perhaps I was going to have to dress up as a fish, but I couldn't swim so I hoped they wouldn't be asking me to do that. It was all very confusing.

'Uncle Douglas is a famous film producer,' she went on. 'He's going to be taking you away for filming for a few days. You'll meet other children.'

She made it sound as though it was a great opportunity for me but I knew from bitter experience that anything involving Uncle Douglas was not going to be good fun. I could be quite sure of that. When he picked me up he didn't take me to the hotel as usual – instead he drove me to his house. It was just the sort of place you would expect such a disgusting man to live in. Tucked away out of sight down at the end of a cul-de-sac, it was separated off from any neighbouring houses by tall dark trees and high fences. It looked big and dark and forbidding before you even walked through the door.

Inside the gloomy interior the stench of stale food and sweat and dirt was overpowering, making you want to gag. Everything was filthy and the windows were all sealed so that there was no chance of anyone escaping or of any fresh air getting in. The house contained a maze of nasty little rooms. First of all I was led into a sort of sitting room where several other kids were sitting staring at the ground. It was like a sort of holding area and Uncle Douglas explained to me that the rules in there were strict. We weren't allowed to speak to anyone else, not even one another, or to make eye contact. We had to keep our eyes on the floor at all times. I imagine that they were the same rules the slave traders in the seventeenth and eighteenth centuries used in order to ensure their charges didn't mutiny or become bold or defiant.

We were mostly boys, although there were a few girls. The girls were sniffling and sobbing, while the boys were dry-eyed and silent, like the walking dead. I was told that if anyone broke a rule and looked up, or spoke, or refused to do what they were told, or simply got an instruction wrong, they would be taken to the 'punishment room' and beaten savagely until they had learned their lesson.

Douglas was undoubtedly the man in charge of this little kingdom, but he had a sidekick called Joe, who was just as vicious and vile as him. Joe was his assistant, responsible for herding us down corridors when we were needed, or taking us to the punishment room. He must have looked to the outside world like a total misfit, with his grubby black trackie bottoms, white socks and lumpy shoes. If he wore a jumper it always seemed to be too small for him, the sleeves ending inches above his bony wrists. The buttons of his floral shirts would always be undone, showing a disgustingly hairy chest, contrasting with a spookily hairless chin on his drawn, pale face. He was tall and thin, the opposite to fat Douglas. Together they were like a pair of cartoon baddies from a Disney film. They might have been a couple of losers in the world outside the house, but inside it they possessed total power.

To begin with I was relieved to see other people around, especially other kids, thinking perhaps Uncle Douglas would leave me alone if he didn't have the privacy he needed to indulge his appetites. I soon realized that everyone in the house was there for the same reason and he wasn't going to have to keep anything hidden or private. Out in the hallway I heard some adult voices and it wasn't long before I became aware that these were the clients who would be paying for our services.

The men who came to the house always looked a little disconcerted when they first walked in and breathed the foul air, and most of them refused Douglas's eager offers of tea from the cracked and stained mugs that festered on every surface, but they always stayed because they knew that he was offering them things that they would have trouble getting anywhere else. He was offering them a walk on the dark side of life, an opportunity to go to places that didn't exist in their normal, respectable, everyday worlds. Sometimes they would discreetly try to open one of the windows to let some air into one or other of the stinking rooms, but none of the hinges moved; they had all been painted over years before.

Uncle Douglas was able to satisfy his customers' most evil fantasies because he had a string of terrified slaves like me, people who had been sold to him by their families or carers and who were too frightened to protest or put up any sort of fight because they knew what would happen to them if they tried. Our spirits had been broken and we had been trained to obey; we knew what was expected of us and we knew we would be brutally punished if we didn't provide it.

Douglas must have felt that he had groomed me well enough and that now I was ready to be used for his business, to become 'a porn star', as Mum put it. I didn't realize it when I first walked into that house, but this was where nearly all my weekends and school holidays would be spent for the next three or four years. I was still only nine years old. There were always several of us kids there at the same time and we would be kept there for entire weekends, often longer during the school holidays. It became the new routine of my life; Uncle Douglas would pick me up after school on a Friday and I would be taken back home again on a Sunday evening so I would be ready to get back to school on the Monday morning.

The punters who came and went during those weekends arrived at the door with their twisted fantasies and paid Douglas to set the scenes up and film them while they did whatever they wanted to us. Sometimes they just wanted to watch us doing things to one another; other times they wanted to be inflicting the pain and suffering themselves. Some of them would want to dress up in all sorts of ridiculous costumes that would have had us laughing if we hadn't been so fearful for our lives. Most of the clients were very different to Douglas and Joe, quite respectable-seeming men, mostly wearing wedding rings. Some of them I knew already from visits to our house, like the policeman with his handcuffs. A lot of them were regulars, coming back week after week. It was as if Douglas had managed to get them hooked on his own particular brand of drug and they just couldn't get enough.

They always knew exactly what they wanted, right down to the expressions they wanted us to have on our faces while we performed the acts and the lighting they preferred on the scenes they constructed. Some of the men instructed kids to call them names like 'Mummy' or 'Daddy', but of course I couldn't do that since I still couldn't talk. Sometimes they would want us boys to perform with older girls and we had to pray that we would get the necessary erections or else we would be punished again for disobeying their orders. Generally we would be expected to follow their directions as exactly as professional actors on a film set, or we would be taken out of the room and beaten until we got it right.

Once or twice at the beginning I didn't understand what they were telling me to do and got it wrong and I soon realized they were willing to be as vicious in their punishments as Mum had ever been. Their favourite trick was to grab our testicles and twist them as hard as they could until we were screaming for mercy. Sometimes I would be slow to understand what it was they wanted me to do for the camera. I don't know if it was to do with my learning difficulties or what it was, but they weren't about to make any allowances for anyone and I would be beaten until I got it right just like the others.

I don't know if the clients always knew how badly we had been beaten in order to make us do what they wanted, or whether they actually managed to convince themselves that we were up for it, believing we came from a dirty sub-human world where such things were normal. It seemed to me that if they had children of their own they wouldn't have associated us with them; it was as though we were from a lower species as far as they were concerned.

By listening to what was going on around me, I worked out that some of the children seemed to be related to one or other of the abusers, and all of them were there with the knowledge and co-operation of at least some members of their family. I never came across a single child who had been abducted or kidnapped; they had always been sold into this slavery by someone who should have been looking after them and protecting them from the world. Some of them were even younger than me, no more than eight years old.

There was one boy who was in his late teens and seemed to be the son of one of the other men who was always there. This boy would do whatever they told him, just like us, but he appeared to enjoy it as much as they did. It was as though he had started out a terrified child, just like me, and had become one of 'them' over the years. I knew that would never happen to me; I would never become like these people. Sometimes the clients would get this lad to coach the rest of us in how to do things right. He reminded me of Larry and Barry and the way they acted at home, relishing the whole thing as if it was the greatest fun in the world.

If we behaved well and did it right we would be rewarded with rests, allowed to go to our cell-like little bedrooms where they would lock us in and bring us cups of milky tea and plates of biscuits or bars of chocolate. When you had spent as many years as I had making bottles of stale water last for days on end, you appreciated tiny gestures like that. It was like rewarding the animals in the circus when they got their tricks right. Sometimes they would bring us sandwiches, although there was often mould on the bread. I used to pick the mould off and eat what was left, grateful to be given anything and always aware that I didn't know how long it would be before we were offered anything else.

They would allow us to bath and clean ourselves as long as we did whatever was required of us, but it was hard to feel clean after being in Douglas's disgusting bathrooms. We didn't get peace in there because they always wanted to come in with us, washing us, playing with us, filming us, photographing us. They never missed an opportunity; even if you were just going for a pee they would want to take a photograph, stage-managing the pictures like professional photographers: 'Go on, pull your pants right down.' The only time a bathroom would be cleaned up was if Douglas was going to be doing some filming in there, and then it would suddenly become spotless.

179

At night we would all be locked into our separate little rooms to sleep and I would be able to hear the men's voices downstairs in the kitchen as they continued talking and laughing into the small hours. Every so often during the night I would be woken by the sounds of footsteps on the stairs. The bolt would slide back on the bedroom door and someone would come in to help themselves in private. Sometimes there would be groups of them, particularly after pub closing times, and they would stumble in together but be too drunk to get erections, which would make them angry and violent, as if it was our fault for not arousing them properly. Sometimes, if we had been good during the day and performed well, Douglas would protect us from too many night-time callers.

'Leave him alone now,' I'd hear him say outside the door. 'Let him get his rest.'

I guess he was just protecting his investments, wanting us to be ready to perform effectively again the next day.

All the men in the house seemed completely confident that they would never be caught. Maybe they even kidded themselves that they weren't really doing anything wrong. One time some of us were actually filmed outside in the garden, which was securely fenced in to make sure we couldn't escape. It's strange to think that normal families must have been living in the houses all around, completely unaware of what was going on just a few yards away from where their children played or slept safely in their bedrooms.

If we didn't do exactly what they wanted us to do during filming we were kept awake, not fed and made to do it again and again until we got it right. Even though the things they made us do were horrible, I knew that by the end of each weekend I would at least be cleaned up and would have had enough to eat and drink, which wouldn't have been the case if I had been at home. It's hard to believe, looking back now, that any child could have a home life so terrible that he would be better treated in a place like Douglas's house, but it was true. By that age I had learned to do whatever I could to survive. I knew what it felt like to be left in the dark without food or clean water for days on end, and I knew that was worse than anything these men could do to me. I had been taught how to survive like any captive animal.

I cherished the times that I was rewarded for good behaviour with a break in a private bedroom. I could lie there and listen to the laughter of the customers coming and going and exchanging views on the videos, although I could still hear the screams of pain from the children in the punishment room whose spirits needed to be broken.

None of the customers ever called us by our names because they needed to think of us as objects not people.

They would never treat us with any courtesy or speak to us about anything; not so much as a 'hello' or a 'how are you'. If we had been animals they probably would have talked to us more than they did. Maybe if they had been forced to think of us as individuals with feelings they wouldn't have been able to inflict so much pain on us and wouldn't have been able to make their fantasies about us into reality.

Because I never dared to look too closely at what was going on between them, it was hard to work out quite how the business side of the operation worked. The men who came for the weekends certainly paid for our services, and I guess they paid again to take away video recordings of their performances, which they could then watch and enjoy all over again at their leisure. I think there were other clients who didn't take part but came and bought the videos for their own purposes. There were always people coming and going, talking about this child or that act, comparing notes, recommending different films, asking for more of the same, as if they were normal movie fans hanging out at their local Blockbusters.

There was another man, with an accent which I now think must have been American, who often came to the house while we were filming but never participated in the scenes himself. Douglas was always very respectful towards him, doing exactly what the man told him, and he would go away again with a bunch of videos. I guess he was some sort of businessman who knew how to sell the material to a wider audience. He always knew exactly what he wanted, like a film producer instructing a director what to film. I presume that when you read in the papers about material being downloaded from the Internet it must come from people like him; maybe he was part of some sort of organized pornography distribution ring.

None of us children knew or cared about things like that; we just cared about how much they were hurting us and how little they were bothered about us as human beings. We were broken creatures, keeping our heads down and getting by as best we could. Occasionally I glanced at one or other of them and made brief eye contact, wondering what their lives were like, but we never dared to flout the rules by talking to each other.

When I was dropped back home from my weekends at Douglas's house, feeling sore and distraught, Mum and Amani would never do anything to make me comfortable or to reward me for earning them so much money. If there were any dirty jobs to be done around the house, like unblocking the toilet, they would have saved them for me, and they'd force my hand down the bowl if I hesitated for even a second. As far as they were concerned I was just a slave, an object to be used whenever needed. They didn't want me getting the idea that I had any rights to special treatment just because I was now 'a porn star'. I was still their property before anything else.

Chapter Twelve

Learning to Speak Again

Sometimes when I went to school on a Monday morning it was only a matter of hours since I had been delivered back from Douglas's house. I would be buried so far inside my own head, trying to protect myself from thinking about everything that had happened to me, trying not to make anyone angry with me, trying to hide from the world, that I would hardly dare to raise my eyes to the blackboard once I was sitting in the classroom. Silent, angry and withdrawn, I must have seemed an impossible challenge for the adults who were trying to help me. They could never have imagined what was churning round inside my head or how much my body hurt after a weekend of abuse by several grown men.

As the teachers laboured to broaden my mind and encourage my creativity, my brain was still numb from the humiliations and terrors I had so recently endured, and which I had every reason to believe I would have to go through again the following weekend, maybe even that evening when I got home.

The authorities were doing their best to help me, believing that they were just dealing with a boy who had been deeply traumatized by the horrific death of his father. My one-to-one teacher in the classroom, Miss Meredith, was a warm, kind, gentle woman in her late twenties whose main task was to help me with my reading and writing. She sat beside me all day through every class and even today I can remember how lovely she smelled when she came close to me, so fresh and clean and scented like flowers. If she tried to hug me I had no idea how to respond, going rigid with fear and embarrassment, which must have made it awkward for her. It had been so long since anyone had touched me with anything other than violence and greed, so long since I had seen anyone treat anyone else with affection.

Her efforts to help me come out of my shell were mostly falling on stony ground. It was as though I was stuck in a mental rut, frightened to poke my head out and risk feeling any new emotions. All I did whenever I was given a pencil and paper was draw pictures of my dad on fire, a little stick figure running frantically around with flames pouring out like angels' wings behind him, because that was all I ever saw when I looked inside my box of memories. Nothing that had happened to me in my life since that day had given me anything happy that I might have been able to replace that hellish image with. All my happy memories had ended at the second the car exploded in the garage, literally going up in flames. Miss Meredith would try to coax me to think of something else I might like to draw a picture of. She would never force me to do anything I didn't want to do; she just encouraged me all the time, which was an experience I had never had with a grown-up before.

'Why don't you draw a house and some trees?' she would ask. 'What about a picture of a cat or a dog? Shall we draw an aeroplane? What about drawing a picture of your mummy that you could take home and give to her?'

My speech therapist, Jill, was another extremely kind woman wanting to do her best to help me to break out of my silent mental prison. I was almost nine when we started working together and with her patient encouragement I was soon forcing out more individual one-syllable words but I still couldn't string them into any sort of understandable sentence. She and I knew what the various grunts and gurgles were meant to represent, but if I had tried them on any of my classmates they would just have laughed at me and called me new names. She would show me pictures and try to get me to draw and talk about what I could see, hoping to reopen the pathways between what I saw and heard and what I said. When she realized how serious the blockage was between my brain and my mouth, Jill showed me some exercises I could do with my tongue and my lips in order to form the right sounds. I had to make different noises while she held my tongue down uncomfortably with a spatula. At times I wanted to give up and run away. If she hadn't been so patient and understanding I would never have got through those early sessions.

The first proper word that I coughed out was 'fuck', which made her jump and her eyebrows rise. In those days it was still a rarely used swear word in polite circles, but it was a word I had heard repeated around me more often than any other, and it also expressed very succinctly how I was feeling. And it was an easy one to get my tongue round.

'Oh,' she said, recovering herself quickly. 'Well, you know that word then.'

It was almost as if I had cleared a blockage that day and other words started to come tumbling out, initially indistinct and falling over one another but growing clearer over the following months as the muscles in my tongue, throat and lips began to regain their strength.

'Me,' I would say proudly, 'Joe.'

For a long time I had trouble with the first letters of words. 'Dog' would come out as 'og' and Jill would have to show me physically how to make the 'd' sound in order to complete the word. I must have been using all the wrong muscles because my neck swelled up with the effort of speaking and my throat became sore from the strain of getting those few words out distinctly. Talking is a function that most of us take for granted every day of our lives, but when you are trying to relearn the knack of it from scratch it's an incredibly complex and difficult task.

From single words we moved on to stories. Jill would show me pictures of scenes and ask me what was happening.

'Mum home?' I would suggest.

'Mummy came through the door,' Jill corrected, coaxing me to try to construct whole sentences, 'then went through to the kitchen and made tea.'

'Mum come home. Tea.'

Years of silence meant that finding single words was hard enough without worrying about how to make them flow together. It was like learning a foreign language, putting together single chunks of vocabulary, hoping they would make sense to the listener, but forgetting how to make the links that give subtleties and nuances to anything we have to say to one another.

Jill was endlessly patient, building my voice back one brick at a time. But it wasn't just talking that was a problem for me when it came to fitting in with normal society. Because I was so unpractised in all the social skills other children would take for granted, as well as having muscles that hadn't been exercised in years, my eating habits were messy and my physical co-ordination was terrible. Having grown used to licking scraps of food off the floor, or picking at them with my fingers, I had only a sketchy idea of how to use a knife and fork or a spoon. Miss Meredith had to teach me those sorts of basic life skills as well as the mental skills I needed like reading, writing and maths. I kept remembering Wally telling me I was a bright kid and I would do well one day, but it didn't feel that way as I struggled to master even the simplest skills, the sorts of things other kids would have mastered in their first couple of years at school.

I wanted to learn as much new stuff as I could, but sometimes the effort of just keeping up with the others was almost unbearable and the humiliation of constantly failing to reach even my own modest goals was agonizing. Most children don't remember when they mastered the basic skills of life, and almost assume that they have had them forever. What normal person can remember the first time they successfully tied a tie or brushed their own teeth or managed to eat some peas off a plate using only a knife and fork? Well, I do.

Mum convinced the teachers that all my problems stemmed from my development being delayed by the shock of seeing Dad on fire, my 'tilted brain' as she put it so bizarrely. It was an impression that I reinforced by continually drawing pictures of the accident, colouring the flames in with bright oranges, yellows and reds, pressing down so hard I wore the crayons away. I was obviously obsessed by that one terrible moment in my life and had never been able to go through the normal grieving and recovery processes. Most children subjected to such a trauma would have had counselling and therapy and would have been treated with gentleness and respect while they tried to find their balance in the world once more. Quite the opposite had happened to me; nothing good had happened since and no caring adult had even tried to replace those terrible images of my father running around the garage on fire.

Mum had lengthy and charming answers for any questions the authorities might put to her, and she was so practised at delivering these explanations they always sounded completely plausible. When they asked why I ate my food like an animal, she told them she had tried to teach me table manners but that I had refused to use implements to eat, just grabbing aggressively at any food that was put in front of me and throwing the cutlery around the room. She didn't tell them that she had often not given me any food at all for days on end, or that she had made me eat off the floor or out of a dog's bowl. Sometimes when I listened to her explaining everything away I found it difficult to believe my own memory of events, but then as soon as she got me home again it would all come rushing back when she once again turned into the monster I had always known.

But despite all the disappointments and set-backs, the hard work that Miss Meredith and the teachers were putting in was starting to have an effect. Free of my cell and allowed at least a few hours of mental stimulation each day in an atmosphere where I could feel safe and relatively sure no one was going to attack me beyond a bit of childish teasing, things which had seemed like a meaningless blur to me when I first walked into the classroom began to come into focus and make a sort of hazy sense. Very slowly, as the months went by, I started to catch up with the other children – although they were always able to move ahead more quickly when we were given new things to learn, because their knowledge was based on more solid foundations than mine.

Jill's efforts were also paying off and by the time I was due to move on to secondary school at the age of eleven, I was starting to be able to string full sentences together. But still the words I needed would desert me unexpectedly if I was under any sort of pressure and I would be left stuttering around in search of them.

It was a huge relief when the first sentences came out and I could see that other people had heard me and understood what I was saying. Being able to communicate almost freely with the world around me was like being unlocked from a prison inside my head. For the first time in years the outside world could actually hear what I had to say, could know what I was thinking and feeling. I was no longer just a silent object, an embarrassment in social situations, a problem to teachers and social workers. I could respond to things people said to me, try out ideas on people and attempt to make them laugh. That was the best feeling, because if people were laughing they weren't hitting me and there was always a chance they would like having me around, wanting me to entertain them some more. At last I could answer people's questions if I wanted to, although most of the things that were stored in my head I didn't want to share with anyone.

The fact that I was starting to talk and going to school like a normal child didn't make any difference to my situation once I got home in the afternoons. If anything, Mum became even stricter in order to ensure she kept me in my place now that there was a possibility I could talk to other people or write or draw descriptions of my life during the years in the cellar. She could no longer rely on my muteness to protect her from discovery. She had to ensure that I was never in any doubt what would happen to me if I didn't obey her every word or if I ever tried to get her into trouble. She didn't have to worry; I still believed she was capable of killing me if she felt she had to, or if I provoked her temper far enough. I was still more frightened of her than of anyone or anything else.

As soon as I walked in through the door after school she would order me to strip down to my underpants and I would be sent up to the bedroom to sit and do nothing until she or one of the others told me to do otherwise. It was hard to know what was worse – the hours of boredom when I just stared at the hands on the clock, or the things they would make me do, whether dirty jobs around the house, or disgusting sexual acts with Amani or my brothers.

Even though the other kids at school could now understand some of the things I was saying, I was still considered a bit of a freak – but at least now I was just 'the boy with the speech impediment' rather than the boy who 'didn't talk'. In the mid 1980s, school authorities were starting to hire more teachers to help children who had special needs and I was given more support than I would have been even a few years before.

I still wasn't an easy child for anyone to deal with. The words that came most easily to my lips were phrases like 'fuck off' and 'you c***', sayings that I had heard repeated over and over again throughout my life, literally having them beaten into me day and night. Swearing and snarling at anyone who tried to help me also allowed me to vent my own anger and frustration at the world.

One of the many reasons why I was so disruptive was because I was frustrated by my own inability to do most of the schoolwork I was given. After a couple of years I no longer had Miss Meredith to guide me. Once I had mastered the basics and could talk and read and write, they assumed I could keep up on my own but I would sometimes find myself losing control as I struggled to make sense of what the teachers were saying and writing up on their blackboards.

At the age of eleven we all moved on to senior school, even though I had only received two years of education by then and was woefully ill-equipped to cope. Just when I thought I was getting a grip on something, the teachers would move on to something else. Everyone else in the class had got the hang of it before me and I would be far too self-conscious to ask them to stop and go over it again for me. After a while I would give up even trying and I would start messing around to cover up my own failures, flicking things around the room with my ruler or pulling stupid faces, no longer listening to anything the teacher was saying.

I wanted to win as many friends and be as popular as possible and the best way to do that was to make the other kids laugh at every opportunity. I was always easily led astray, just as I had been when Larry and Barry played tricks on me in the bedroom getting me to do things that would annoy Mum. Anything the other kids dared me to do, I would immediately do simply to please them and make them like me. If they told me to throw something at the teacher's back while he was working on the board I would do it, just to please them. This meant I was constantly getting into trouble and being punished. Compared to the punishments I received at home, however, there was nothing they could do to me at school that was too frightening. The worst thing they could threaten me with was telling Mum what I was getting up to, because then she would give me one of her batterings once she got me home.

Most of the people who had given me a hard time at my old school had gone to other secondary schools so I had an opportunity to make a new set of friends who didn't have any preconceptions about me. Pete had come to the same school as me but he was in different classes because he was one of the clever ones whereas I was struggling to keep up at all. We remained good friends, though, and I grew to trust him enough to tell him a little about what went on in our house. I didn't tell him about the sex, because that was too embarrassing, but when I described the violence he told me in no uncertain terms that I should report it to someone and get help. He said that there were helplines for kids to ring if they were being mistreated by their parents, and he told me the phone number of one of them, but I didn't think it could possibly do any good to talk to people like that. Pete came from such a different world that he couldn't imagine why I wouldn't be able to just tell the authorities –

that was the sort of thing his parents would have known all about – but I was never going to be able to do it.

Even though I knew Pete didn't really understand, I trusted him completely not to pass my secrets on. He had no trouble believing that I was telling the truth because he had experienced Mum in a hostile mood that time he came to our door. I don't know how he would have reacted if I had told him everything; he probably would have forced me to talk to the authorities about it, or maybe he'd have told his parents.

Because I didn't talk about it to anyone I assumed that most children had to put up with some sort of sexual interference in their family lives. I didn't think the violence we endured at home was normal because I had seen that other children weren't frightened of their parents, but I didn't know what went on inside the privacy of their family bedrooms. I assumed lots of adults used the children in their families for sexual relief.

Sexual matters are confusing enough for any young boy as he starts to experience urges that would have been entirely alien to him just a year or two before, but for me it was even more of a puzzle. I was filled with a mixture of fear, guilt and my own growing desires. The only thing I was sure of was that I found girls attractive, not boys or men. But having been subjected to such a variety of extreme sexual acts by so many different people from an early age I had no idea where the barriers were

supposed to stand between appropriate and inappropri-
ate behaviour.

Once, when I was thirteen, I got over-enthusiastic
and touched a girl at school inappropriately, without
thinking for a second that I was doing anything wrong.
She immediately went to a teacher and told on me and I
got hauled in front of the headmaster. He explained to
me that boys just mustn't do those sorts of things,
however much they might want to. I couldn't understand what the big fuss was about, because it had only
been a passing touch and I had come from a world where
everyone took whatever they wanted, regardless of other
people's feelings.

I was horrified when I realized how seriously I had
sinned in the eyes of the girl as well as the headmaster,
and terrified when he told me that Mum had been called
to the school as a result of my 'disgusting' behaviour.

As usual, when she arrived Mum was acting the role
of the perfect, put-upon and slightly puzzled parent,
unable to understand how her child could have let her
down so badly. I sat beside her with my head down and
eyes to the floor, not daring to speak, knowing that I was
going to receive a terrible beating for this once she got
me home – not because she would think anything much
about the degree of the crime, but because she would be
furious to have been called in and embarrassed in front
of the headmaster.

'I don't know where he could have learned such behaviour,' she said and I kept staring at the floor, bursting to blurt out everything that I knew and exactly how I had learned it, but knowing my life wouldn't be worth living if I did. Even now that I was thirteen and no longer a small child, my mother's secrets were still safe with me. Would anyone have believed such tales of horror anyway?

Chapter Thirteen

A Bid for Freedom

One morning, during the year when I was thirteen, Pete came into school with some terrible news.

'My mum and dad have decided to send me to a grammar school,' he told me.

It seemed they had decided that our school wasn't getting the best out of him or something, so he was moving on to try to fulfil his potential somewhere else. Maybe they still thought I was a bad influence and it was me they were trying to separate him from. I didn't know what a grammar school was, but I did know that I probably wouldn't be seeing Pete any more once he'd gone there. I assumed that he would almost certainly just disappear out of my life in the way that Wally had, however much he might protest to the contrary. The idea of losing my one good friend seemed unbearable and I broke down in front of him, crying like a baby –

something I don't think I would have done in front of anyone except him or Wally.

'I can't manage without you,' I sobbed.

'Yeah you can, we'll stay in touch,' he promised, trying to soften the blow, trying to sound casual about the whole thing, as though it was no big deal.

'No, you won't,' I said. 'You say you will, but you won't, not once you have new friends.'

'I will,' he protested, but I could see that he was no more convinced of the truth of that than I was.

I didn't blame him for moving on. I just knew he wouldn't keep in touch and I didn't want to be left hanging around waiting for him to get in contact, as I had for so long with Wally. That had been such a huge let-down that I still couldn't think about it without feeling deeply hurt. I didn't want to be the one who was chasing after Pete and constantly finding he was too busy with his new friends or with his homework or his important exams to be able to spend time with me. I knew only too well how painful it was to hold out hope for something and then to be disappointed yet again. I preferred to face the truth at the beginning, make a clean break and cope with it as best I could. I had to accept that I was going to lose Pete, my only real friend, and that was the end of it.

It was a Monday morning when he broke the news and his words kept going round and round in my head as I sat in my early lessons. I was in a state of shock, even less able to concentrate on anything the teachers were saying than usual. Pete was the only good thing in my life and I couldn't see any point in continuing to go to school without him there. I didn't need him to protect me from the bullies any more, but I knew that I wasn't gaining anything from the classes because I was falling so far behind, so if I couldn't hang out with Pete between classes it all seemed like a big waste of time. As long as I was still in school I had to go home every night to the nightmare of my family life, but if I left school I just might be able to walk away from my whole life: Mum, Amani, Larry, Barry and the vile Uncle Douglas. It was as though a light bulb had suddenly gone on in my head as I began to think practically about running away from school and home and my entire past.

I'd thought about running away before, of course, a million times – especially when I had been lying in the cellar at home or in one of the little bedrooms at Douglas's house. But I had never been able to think of a concrete plan of how to do it or where to go. I'd never actually thought I would get away with it and I knew that when I was inevitably brought back by the police I would be bound to have to face terrible consequences, so I had never found the nerve to go through with it. Having Pete's friendship during school weekdays had been just enough to keep me from having a go. But now that restraint was being lifted, and I was getting older. I was a teenager, so was it really such an unreasonable idea to start my adult life a bit early?

I felt a rising beat of excitement in my heart as the idea blossomed into a definite plan. When I was a small child I'd known I would be caught quickly and taken straight back to Mum, who would have beaten me to a pulp for daring to do such a thing, but I wouldn't be so conspicuous on the streets now that I was older, and I would be able to look after myself better. At least I could talk now, and being friends with Pete had taught me a lot about being more confident in the world. I reasoned that if I could just keep myself hidden and out of everyone's way for a few years I would be old enough to stay away from home legally. I would be free to live my own life, away from all the people who wanted to hurt me and keep me as their slave. How could life on the run be any worse than life at home and at Uncle Douglas's, even if I was forced to live rough for a while? If I could survive for three years in a cellar, surely I could survive anywhere?

Once the idea had taken root it suddenly seemed like the obvious way out of everything that made my life a misery. I decided to act immediately. I didn't want to endure another night of humiliation, pain and abuse at home if I didn't have to; in fact, the idea of going home ever again suddenly seemed intolerable compared with the temptation of the big wide outside world. I knew that I would have an hour at dinnertime when no one would notice I had gone; that would be my chance to get away.

'I've got to go home,' I told Pete when we met as usual after the last morning lesson. 'I don't feel well.'

'Who's coming to get you?' he asked. 'The bitch?'

He'd always referred to Mum in that way, ever since she'd told him to 'fuck off out of it' at our front door.

'Yeah,' I lied. 'Will you tell the teachers for me?'

'Sure,' he shrugged. Maybe he could tell I was acting strangely but if he could, he probably put it down as my reaction to his news.

I went into the dinner room and collected together as much food as I could carry without drawing attention to myself, stuffing it into my pockets while no one was looking. I then strolled as casually as I could manage from the dinner room to the cloakroom and went through everyone's pockets and bags looking for cash. I also scooped up any items of clothing that I thought would be useful once I had discarded my school uniform. I felt guilty about stealing from the other kids but I had gone into survival mode and I knew I wouldn't last long on the run without any money, and I couldn't walk about in my school uniform or I would be hauled over and asked some questions.

When I was ready, I strolled out of the school gates as calmly as my thumping heart would let me, and just kept walking without looking back. I kept on going for hours, putting as many miles as possible between me and my past, marching away from the built-up areas and out into the countryside to a beautiful area well known to holidaymakers during the summer. Campers, tourists and hikers all came to this part of the world in summer but I was pretty sure there was no chance of me bumping into anyone I knew since it was only March.

I'd studied some survival books in the library when I had first learned to read, fantasizing about surviving in the wild somewhere on my own, living on my wits, and I imagined I had learned enough to be able to get away with it. My plan was to build a camp in the woods somewhere and live like Tarzan did in the movies – maybe even making friends with the animals as he did. Animals would be a lot more reliable than people had ever turned out to be. Any hardships I might face in the wild were going to be nothing compared to what I had survived at home, I was sure of that. The further I got from home, the more optimistic I felt that I was going to get away with it, that all my pain and suffering were finally over. I was a free man now and I could put my childhood behind me as I got on with the rest of my life.

By seven o'clock that evening I felt I had walked far enough to be safe from anyone who might by now be searching for me and I began to look around for somewhere to sleep for my first night. I was passing an isolated group of big detached houses when I came across about a dozen kids playing together after their tea. It was nice to see some friendly faces, people who knew nothing about me or my past, and I stopped to talk to them. They were very posh, their voices much more like Pete's than like mine. Their houses looked like mansions to me.

'Where are you from?' a boy who introduced himself as John asked.

'I'm just visiting the area,' I said vaguely.

'Why have you got a bag?' he asked, gesturing at my school backpack, which now held all my worldly possessions.

'None of your business,' I replied.

'Do you want to play football?' he said, changing the subject without seeming in the least put out by my surliness.

'Okay.'

I accepted the invitation readily, hungry for any company and friendship I could find. It felt nice to be with a group of kids who accepted me without knowing anything about my background. They didn't know me as the smelly, mute boy who couldn't read or write very well for his age. To them I was just an interesting stranger who had wandered into their comfortable, secluded little world. They actually seemed to like me for myself. They tried asking me more questions and I managed to make my answers vague enough to sound convincing and friendly without giving anything away.

'Are you going to be here tomorrow?' John asked when it was finally too dark to see the football and it came time for them to go home for the night.

'Yes,' I said, thinking this would be as good a place as any to stop for a while, especially if it meant I had a ready-made group of friends.

'We'll see you then.'

Once they'd gone, shouting their goodbyes, waving cheerily as they ran off into the darkness, the night suddenly seemed very quiet and the air uncomfortably cold. Being out under the immense night sky was a daunting feeling since I had spent so much of my life trapped in confined spaces, but the feeling of liberation was exciting at the same time. The illuminated windows of the big, solid-looking homes that my new friends had disappeared into seemed very tempting as I turned and walked away into the deepening gloom to look for some-where to spend the night. I could see I wasn't going to have time to build myself a shelter as I'd sort of imagined I would, but I would still need to find some protection from the cold. Winter hadn't long passed, and the air was already losing its daytime heat.

My way was lit only just enough by the stars and moon for me to be able to see the world in silhouette around me, but I found a railway line and decided to follow the tracks to make sure I didn't get too lost in the dark shadows of the surrounding trees. I had brought a torch with me, which I had found in someone's bag in the school cloakroom, but I didn't want to use up the batteries unnecessarily, since I didn't know how long it would be before I got a chance to replace them. I was also nervous about drawing attention to my presence there.

I had only gone a couple of hundred yards from the houses when I came across a workman's hut by the side of the track. The door wasn't locked so I pushed my way in, shining the torch around the dusty interior. The beam picked up some old bits of equipment, most of which looked as if it had been long forgotten, and some stored railway sleepers, giant blocks of solid wood which looked as though they had been left there since the lines were first laid. I doubted if anyone used the hut any more, especially at night. It smelled strongly of tar and oil but I had slept amongst far worse smells than that in my time. Perfect, I thought. My own little home in the wild. I pushed the door shut behind me, pulled away some of the cobwebs and managed to find myself a dry corner where I could lie down. I'd been walking for seven hours and then played football so it wasn't long before I fell into a deep sleep, only occasionally woken by the cold.

When the daylight finally returned and I poked my nose out round the door, the countryside was just as deserted as it had been when I went to bed. The only sounds came from the wind and birds in the trees. I decided to explore and went to hide my backpack in some nearby woods, not wanting to carry it around but fearing that some workmen might come to the hut during the day and find it if I left it there. It contained all the possessions I had in the world so I couldn't afford to lose it.

My newfound friends were in school during the day so I passed the long hours playing on my own in the woods. I enjoyed my newfound freedom but I'd finished all the food I'd brought with me from the school dinner room and hunger pains were growling ominously in my stomach like an approaching thunderstorm. All day I was looking forward to seeing John and the other kids when they came out again after school and I was waiting outside their houses for ages before they finally appeared. When John and his sister emerged through their gates I could see that they were looking for me, hoping I would be there, eager to talk, which was a nice feeling.

'What house are you staying at?' John asked as we sat waiting for the others to join us. 'Because we know everyone in the area.'

'Over there,' I said, waving in a vague direction, eager to change the subject.

'But last night you said it was over there,' he protested, obviously puzzled and intrigued at the same time.

'It's a farm over the bridge,' I said, because I had passed several in my journey.

'Which one?' his sister was intrigued now too. 'Our mum and dad know all the farmers.'

Obviously they had been talking about me at home and their parents had shown an interest. I began to feel a little panicked but forced myself to stay calm.

'Okay,' I said, unable to think of any way out. 'I'll be straight with you. Promise me you won't say anything to anyone?'

They nodded solemnly, their eyes wide in anticipation of hearing something amazing. Everyone loves to be told a secret.

'I'm a runaway.'

It was the first time I had actually said the word out loud and the dramatic sound of it quite surprised me.

They both gasped and there was a moment's silence as they took in this astounding fact, followed by a torrent of questions.

'Why?'

'Where are you from?'

'Who have you run away from?'

'Where are you sleeping?'

'What are you going to do now?'

I explained that my mum hurt me and was threatening to kill me.

'If they find me,' I said, 'the police will take me back home and she will really hurt me.'

211

I made them swear over and over again not to tell anyone, not even the other members of their gang – but not surprisingly it was too juicy a piece of news for them to be able to keep it to themselves and within five minutes of turning up all the other kids in the group knew about it. I guess every child must dream about running away from home at one time or another, and now they had met someone who had actually done it and they wanted to be part of the adventure themselves. Football was forgotten – they just wanted to sit around and talk and plan my future with me. Everyone was talking at once.

'Okay,' John said after a while, 'we'll make a pact. We won't tell anyone, and we'll look after you.'

We moved further away from the houses to be sure we wouldn't be overheard and they got me to sit down and tell them more about the things Mum did to me. They listened with their jaws hanging open. I didn't tell them about anything sexual, just the beatings and about being locked in a room with no light or food for days on end. It was obvious none of them had ever even realized there was such a thing as child abuse; none of them could even imagine having a mother like mine. She must have sounded like a character from a horror movie, which pretty much sums up what she was like. I could see they were deeply shocked and that they truly did want to do something to help.

'So where did you stay last night?' John's sister wanted to know

I pointed down the track to the hut.

'But wasn't it really cold in there?'

I shrugged and nodded. 'It was a bit.'

'I'll tell you what we'll do.' She was taking charge of the situation now. 'We'll go home and steal you some blankets.'

'No, I've got a better idea,' John overrode her in his enthusiasm. 'We'll sneak you into our house and you can hide out under my bed. We can bring you downstairs and feed you whenever my mum and dad go out.'

I was really beginning to panic now. If we started doing all these things it wouldn't be long before a grown-up suspected what was going on and asked some serious questions. These kids didn't look like the sorts that would stand up well under interrogation. They were treating the whole thing as a glorified game, like any child from a normal background would, but to me it was deadly serious, a matter of life and death. If I was caught and taken home now I was pretty sure Mum would lose the plot completely and might very well kill me in her next explosion of temper.

'I don't think that would work,' I said, not wanting to sound ungrateful. 'But I am quite hungry.'

'Okay,' John said, jumping up, 'we'll get you a feast.'

213

'Don't go mad,' I said. 'Don't take anything anyone will miss. We don't want to arouse their suspicions.'

Despite me pleading with them to show some restraint they had decided what they wanted to do and were too excited to be reasoned with. They all dashed off back to their homes, telling me to wait for them in my hut.

Once inside their houses they went mad, emptying their parents' cupboards, bringing me down armfuls of bedclothes and carrier bags full of food, turning the hut into a little home from home, like a cross between a children's camp and Santa's grotto. Not all of it had been completely thought through – such as the tins of baked beans that came without a tin opener – but there was still enough for me to eat my fill as they babbled on about their plans for my future and how they were going to care for me and hide me. It felt a bit as though I was a pet dog again, but at least now I was a cherished family pet, not a despised one.

'You'll be our best runaway friend,' they said as they proudly showed me everything they had stolen for me, 'and we'll never tell anyone that you're here.'

On their record so far I didn't have too much faith in them being able to keep such an exciting secret from their families for long, but it still felt nice to be the centre of so much friendly attention and I was grateful for the bedclothes and the food. The contrast between the way they were looking after me in that hut, and the way Mum and Amani and the rest of them had looked after me in the past, when I was just a small child, touched me and made me feel sad at the same time. Why didn't my own family want to look after me like this? I decided to stop worrying about things I could do nothing about and just enjoy my good fortune for a few days before moving on. All the bad stuff was behind me now, I reminded myself. I didn't need to think about it any more.

My new friends were obviously nervous about leaving me on my own that night and didn't want to tear themselves away and go back to their houses. I expect they half wanted to camp out with me and share the adventure for a bit longer, but as it grew later I was getting increasingly nervous that their parents would wonder where they were and would come looking for them. I begged them to go back home before that happened.

'What if some strange man comes past and hurts you?' John's sister asked and the others all agreed.

'They won't,' I assured them, desperately wanting them to go now. 'It's dark enough, no one will see me.'

'Wild animals might eat you,' someone else suggested.

'No, really,' I insisted. 'I'll be all right.'

I kept on trying to convince them it was safe to leave me, stressing again how important it was that they didn't tell another soul about me. They promised and I know they did intend to do their best. Eventually they reluctantly agreed to leave me and I settled down under the blankets for a warmer night's sleep than the night before, my stomach feeling comfortably full.

For the next few days my friends came to see me after school each evening, bringing more and more supplies, far more than I needed or could actually eat. On the fifth night John took me to one side and put forward a new proposition.

'Why don't you come and live with us?' he suggested, and I could tell he'd been thinking about it a lot, probably talking it through with his sister. 'You could be my older brother. If I tell my mum and dad that your mum is nasty to you they could adopt you and you could stay with us permanently.'

I couldn't deny that it sounded like a tempting option, but I was old enough and experienced enough to know that the chances of something like that happening were less than slight. I knew Mum would never give me up unless someone paid her enough money to compensate her for her financial losses. I was worth too much to her in potential earnings and she wouldn't want to give me the chance of being happy anyway. I also couldn't imagine that these kids' parents would be too thrilled about taking in a stray child with learning difficulties and a history of behavioural problems just because their own children asked them to.

'No,' I said, more vehemently than I had intended. 'I'm happy here. Honestly.'

That night John decided he needed to get me some hot food for a change. While sitting at the family dinner table he started secretly putting roast potatoes into a bag and then announced he needed to go to the toilet. He dashed down to the hut to give them to me before they went cold but when he returned to the dinner table ten minutes later his mum wanted to know where he'd been.

'I've been in the toilet,' he lied.

'No, you haven't,' she said, 'because I looked. I saw you outside.'

'There was a stray dog out there,' he said, his brain racing to find a convincing cover story. 'I felt sorry for him.'

Despite his quick cover-up, his mother's suspicions had been raised. She had already noticed how many items had been disappearing from the kitchen cupboards over the previous few evenings and obviously felt that she was onto something. She certainly didn't believe that her son was feeding a stray dog with tins of beans, loaves of bread, bottles of milk and packets of cereal. The questions went on and on until eventually my friend's inability to tell bare-faced lies to his own mother got the better of him and he confessed the whole story. I suspect he was relieved to get it off his conscience; he wasn't the sort of boy who would have been comfortable lying to his parents, even if it was in what he thought was a good cause.

I had no idea of any of this as I settled down to sleep for another night in my hut. The first I knew that something was wrong was when I was woken later that night by the sound of footsteps outside, crunching through the shingle on the track. Immediately alert I threw off the stolen bedclothes and knelt by the door, peering out through a crack, my heart pounding as I tried to assess the danger. I could see the beam of a torch coming towards me. The figure holding it looked too tall to be one of the kids, and the footfall was too heavy, more like the scrunch of an adult man's boots. Not sure what to do next, I leaned my whole weight against the door, wedging it with my foot, buying myself a few seconds to think. I assumed it must be a railway maintenance man doing some night work and I began to plan how I would get out the door and past him before he had a chance to grab me and before any of his mates turned up.

The footsteps stopped directly outside the door and a thin slither of torchlight came in through the crack making me instinctively dodge back out of its path.

'Who's in there?' a man's voice enquired. 'Joe, is that you?'

Now I was confused; how did the stranger in the dark know my name?

'I'm a police officer.'

'Fuck off!' I shouted, unable to think of anything intelligent to say in the circumstances. I was thinking about the policeman who used to come to my cellar and to Douglas's house and shivering at the prospect of being arrested and falling back into their hands.

'There's a few people worried about you,' he persisted. His voice sounded kind and concerned but I'd been fooled like that before and I wasn't falling for it again – not now I'd had a taste of freedom.

'Like fuck they are!' I shouted.

'Come on; open the door, Joe, please. I need to see if you're okay.'

'I am, so fuck off.'

'But I need to see for myself that you're all right. Please open the door. I don't want to have to kick it in and hurt you because that wouldn't be nice, would it? I really am a policeman and if you open the door a little you'll be able to see my uniform. These people up here are your friends and they're worried about you.'

'Fucking grasses!' I shouted. 'I don't want to go back. Please, can't you just leave me alone? Forget you even heard about me. Please.'

'I can't lad, no, sorry. My duty is to make sure you are protected.'

I could tell he wasn't going to change his mind and just go away. If I stayed where I was, I was trapped. If he came in, I would be cornered and it would be harder to get away than if I was outside. I made a decision and opened the door, letting him think he had won me over with his reasonableness and his promise of protection. I stepped out with my bag over my shoulder and he took a firm hold of my wrist to make sure I didn't do a runner. I didn't like the feeling after being free for a few days; it reminded me of all the other times I had been gripped by adult hands and pulled in one direction or another, but I didn't struggle. It wouldn't have been worth it and he would only have tightened his hold on me. He was too strong for me to be able to wriggle free; I just had to hope that an opportunity would arise for me to get away before he had me under lock and key. As we made our way up towards the road we had to get over a steep bank. I could tell he was having difficulties, his feet sliding out from under him and only one hand free to support himself when he was in danger of falling.

'You don't have to hold me that hard,' I protested, realizing it was going to be difficult for him to negotiate this obstacle with me attached to him. 'I'm not going anywhere.'

'You're not going to run now, are you?' he asked, sounding a bit doubtful at the prospect of loosening his grip. 'You promise me?'

'No, of course not. I promise you.' Everyone else made promises that they didn't intend to keep, I thought, so why should I be any different? I was willing to do anything I could to stay out of Mum's clutches.

The moment I felt his fingers slacken I tore free and was off into the night. I could hear him shouting after me. 'Joe, come back here.' But I didn't turn round and in my fear and desperation I must have put on a real burst of speed, despite tripping several times on the many unseen obstacles in my path, because I had soon pulled away into the darkness. I left him trailing along behind until eventually even the beam of his torch had disappeared from sight. It's surprising how much energy fear will give you when you need it. I found out later that the police searched for me for the next couple of days, and I did see the odd police car circling around as I watched from my next hiding place, but they didn't seem to be putting their whole hearts into it. I guess they thought I would turn up sooner or later, that I wouldn't have the necessary skills to survive for long in the wild on my own.

Once I was confident I had got away from him I slowed down, stumbling round in circles through the woods until I came into a deserted summer campsite. There I found an empty log cabin that had been locked up for the winter. The lock on the door was flimsy and I managed to force my way in with one hefty kick. It was more comfortable than the previous hut had been; there was even a bed, which I threw myself down onto, my heart pounding from the exertions of the night. The cabin was dry and clean, but it was still cold once I had cooled down again after the running. All my bedclothes had been left behind in the hut and I didn't think it would be wise to go back for anything the next day in case the police were still watching it. I imagined that the kids' families would probably have reclaimed their property by then anyway. I didn't know how long it would be before someone came to open the cabin up for the summer, but I thought it would do as a hideout until the police had stopped bothering to look for me at least.

I stayed in the cabin for several days, living off the remains of the food supplies that I had been keeping in my bag, rationing them out carefully to make them last, seeing no one. The following Sunday I was wandering around the empty campsite for yet another day, keeping myself entertained as best I could. The site had given me a lot of space and quiet to be alone with my own thoughts. I was used to being on my own, so that wasn't a problem. I was content to mooch around looking for things to salvage and things to eat with nobody else to interfere with me or boss me about. I wasn't giving the future too much serious thought, but I suppose I imagined I would just keep moving from place to place over the coming years, scrounging enough food to survive as I went, maybe getting the odd job here and there for pocket money. Being alone in the woods was so much better than being at home, or spending the weekend at Douglas's house, that I didn't give much thought to anything else. If I let myself think about it, I missed Pete and I sometimes wondered what was happening to my brother Thomas. We were never bosom buddies the way I was with Pete, but I knew he had a bad time at home and I worried about him.

It was evening and the light was beginning to fade when I heard some kids' voices in the woods close to the cabin. I dived back inside and watched through the corner of the window to see if they had any adults with them. When they came into sight I saw it was John and his sister, who I guessed had been the ones to grass on me. I should have kept quiet and waited for them to move on but I felt so angry with them for telling the grown-ups about me being in the railway hut after all the promises they had made that I couldn't stop myself from going out to give them a piece of my mind. Maybe I needed someone to talk to as well, wanting to alleviate the boredom and loneliness a bit.

They nearly jumped out of their skins when I suddenly appeared on the path in front of them.

'Why did you grass on me?' I demanded. 'You said you wanted to be my friend and to persuade your family to adopt me as your brother and then you go and fucking grass on me!'

'I was worried about you,' John said, obviously excited to have found me again but nervous about how I would react to them. He didn't want to scare me away again. 'But you got away. They're looking everywhere for you. There's been a big search party and everything.'

I couldn't stay mad at them for long and once I had calmed down they promised that this time they really wouldn't tell anyone about where I was – but I knew I couldn't trust them. I couldn't trust anyone and every time I forgot that rule I ended up being let down again.

'Can we get you any food or blankets?' he asked.

'Just leave me alone,' I said, not wanting to push my luck.

I could see they weren't going to do that, however much I pleaded. It was still all too much of an adventure for them, and they did seem to be genuinely concerned about me.

'I'll tell you what,' I said, 'go back and get me some food then.'

'You stay here with Joe,' John told his sister, 'and I'll go back.' I guess he didn't trust me either and was worried I would run away again the moment they were gone.

'They'll know if you come back without me and take food,' his sister said. 'They'll expect us to be together.'

'Okay,' he said, doubtfully. 'Promise you won't go anywhere, Joe?'

'I promise,' I lied.

The moment they were out of sight I grabbed my bag and ran off into the woods. There was no one in the world I was going to trust any more if it meant I might be taken back home. It wasn't that I doubted their good intentions; I just thought there would be a strong chance the adults would be watching them and would immediately work out what was going on if they saw more food disappearing from the house. I was going to have to stay on my own if I wanted to be safe; there was no other option. This was how my life was going to have to be until I was old enough for the police not to be bothered about me any more.

Chapter Fourteen

Betrayal and Capture

The moment I was back out in the open I immediately missed the protective walls of the log cabin. The outdoor life can seem very alluring when you are trapped inside places that are making you miserable, but nature has an unkind way of reminding you why the human race has mostly chosen to live in houses throughout history. As the last of the daylight disappeared it started to rain hard. The water soaked through my clothes within minutes and kept on coming. A wind sprang up, driving the rain horizontally into my face as I walked, chilling every inch of me down to my bones. As I stumbled around in the dark, feeling cold, tired, wet and hungry, I kept thinking about John and the other kids going back to their warm houses and happy families and it all seemed so unfair.

I felt a surge of bitterness and anger at the way my life had gone; why couldn't I have a normal life like everyone else? Why had God always had it in for me from the day I was conceived by mistake after that bloody anniversary party? Why had he taken my dad away and given him to the devil and never given me a single lucky break since? As I plodded through the wet with my head down against the elements I was raging and cursing Him out loud. It was as if I was making up for all the years when my anger and unhappiness had been trapped behind my silence. Anyone coming across me that night would have thought that they had found a deranged madman ranting in the woods – and in a way they would have been right.

I didn't know where to go or which direction to head in. I wanted to find somewhere dry where I could lie down and sleep but I couldn't think of anywhere to go that would be safe. There was nowhere people wouldn't come searching for me, nowhere I would just blend in without people asking questions and telling others about me. It felt as though the whole world was joined together in an enormous conspiracy against me, a gigantic spider's web with all of the strands trying to pull me back to Mum, while she sat in the centre waiting patiently for me to land in her lap again.

I thought about trying to find my way back to the railway hut and staying there to dry out before slipping away again first thing in the morning. But I decided it was likely the police would go back to look for me at some stage, particularly if John and the others told them they had spotted me again and they knew I was still in the area.

Although the rain started letting up a bit after an hour or two everything was still drenched in the woods, and the trees dripped on me as I passed underneath them. Every part of my body was aching with exhaustion and cold but there was nowhere to sit or lie or take shelter. It made any ideas I might ever have had of living rough in the woods seem like the ridiculous little boy's fantasies that they were. Eventually I walked out from under the dripping trees onto a deserted road so that I could at least put one foot in front of the other without tripping over roots and fallen branches, banging my shins and twisting my ankles every few steps. I knew from my earlier explorations of the area that there was a little local supermarket about three miles up the road so I headed for that, thinking that perhaps there would be somewhere to shelter around it. I thought I could remember seeing a public phone box on the road outside it and another idea was beginning to ferment inside my head.

Although I needed to be alone in order to feel at all safe, the trouble with having so much time to myself was that it had allowed memories that I would normally have suppressed to bob back to the surface. The more I remembered what had happened to me in my short life the angrier I became and the more certain that it couldn't be right. For so many years I had assumed that most children had to put up with at least some of the things that I had been through, but now I was growing older and getting a better idea of what other people's lives were like, I could see more and more clearly that that wasn't true. I might have been angry with Pete for leaving the school, and I might have been angry with my new friend John for telling on me, but the small glimpses they had allowed me of their lives made me realize that my life wasn't normal. I could see how shocked they had been by even the small amounts of information I had given them about my family, so there must be other people out there who would feel the same if they just knew what my situation was. Maybe, I thought, I didn't have to struggle on alone. Maybe there were some good people out there somewhere who would help me if I went to them and explained everything that had been going on. I couldn't trust the police because of the policeman who came to Uncle Douglas's, but perhaps there were other organizations. My brain churned over and over as I walked on, my cold, wet clothes chafing my skin, making every step a misery.

I remembered Pete telling me that there were telephone numbers for kids to ring if they were being

treated badly by their families. I'd never thought of
ringing one before because I had been told so often by
Mum and Amani and Douglas that no one would ever
believe anything I said that I had actually come to
believe it was a fact. Mum had always been so convincing in her lies whenever the authorities had questioned
or challenged her that I always assumed they would
believe her and deliver me back to her if I tried to go for
help. I was so terrified to think what she would do to me
if she got her hands on me after I had tried to betray her
that I never had the nerve to try it. But now that I had
thought it through more thoroughly, and had been safe
from her for more than a week, I was beginning to
think about things a bit differently. Pete had believed
everything I'd told him, and so had John and the kids
who had wanted to look after me, so perhaps other
people would too.

Now that I had time to reflect on everything that had
happened to me over the previous eight or so years I
began to realize that my case must be extreme. If Pete
and John and the others were all so shocked by the little
bits of my life that I had revealed to them, I couldn't
begin to imagine how they would react if they knew the
whole truth. Maybe people on a phone line would believe
me and help me too, just like Pete and the kids by the
railway line. But which people would be the best to turn
to? As far as I was concerned they were all strangers who

had the potential to do me harm if I was unlucky in my choice.

There was one telephone number that Pete had told me several times that I should ring and I could remember it because it was deliberately catchy to make it memorable. As it kept going round and round in my head I began to wonder if perhaps Pete was right. Maybe these were the people who would understand what I was going through if I told them, people with enough experience to know that I was telling the truth, people who would have the ability to protect me from Mum and Amani and Douglas. The idea was becoming more tempting as I squelched on down the dark, cold, empty road.

When I got to the little country supermarket, on the empty, isolated road, I climbed straight into the phone box just to get out of the rain and give myself a few moments to think what to do next. Being so cold and wet and hungry made me acutely aware that I wasn't going to be able to cope on my own indefinitely. I was going to have to find someone I could trust who could help me and protect me from Mum and the rest of them. As I stood there, shivering, staring around me, water dripping down my neck from my soaked hair, I spotted a card pinned to the board above the phone, advertising the same helpline number that Pete had told me about. It was like a sign, as though God or someone was trying to tell me what to do next. Even then it still took me a while to pluck up the courage to lift the receiver and my heart was thumping in my ears as I dialled clumsily with my frozen fingers.

The line rang for a long time but no one answered so after a few minutes I hung up, part of me grateful to have been given a way out of having to find the words to describe to a stranger what my life was like. My nerve was failing me again. What if the people at the other end of the phone rang the police and they sent me back to Mum? There was every possibility she would kill me for running away. But if I didn't get help I was likely to die of cold and hunger anyway. I stood there for a long time, trying to calm myself down and then picked up the receiver and dialled again. Still no answer after the first few rings. I hung up and dialled several more times, my nerve going each time before anyone answered. How could I trust anyone when everyone had always betrayed me, abused me or left me? Dad had gone, Wally had gone, Pete had gone, my friends by the railway line had told on me. What made me think these people would be any different? But outside it was pitch black and the rain was growing heavy again. What other option did I have? I couldn't spend the rest of my life hiding in a phone box. I dialled again and a woman answered the phone in a quiet, sweet voice before I had time to hang up.

I couldn't find the words to speak, just standing there as mute as I'd been all those years before, my throat tightly closed and my brain unable to think what to do about it.

'Are you still on the line?' she asked after a moment. 'Can I help you?'

'I'm being hit by my mum,' I mumbled eventually.

'Okay,' she said, as though that was the most reasonable thing in the world for me to tell her. 'Where are you calling from now?'

'Why?' I asked, immediately suspicious and half wanting to run back out into the rain again.

'I just need to know if you are in a safe place. Are you calling from someone's house?'

'No, a phone box.'

'It's quite late at night, so have you come out of your house?'

'No, I've fucking run away!' I was getting annoyed and knew I had to make a conscious effort to calm down if I was to expect her to help me.

'Oh, all right.' She didn't seem perturbed by my attitude or my swearing. Maybe my call wasn't so unusual and she was used to dealing with fear and aggression in the kids that rang up. 'How long have you run away for?'

'What's with all the questions?' I wanted to know. 'What are you going to do to help me?'

'First of all we need to know your name.'

'Why?'

'I need to know what to call you. My name is Susan, what's yours?'

I didn't answer immediately. I was beginning to worry that I was making a mistake, but at the same time it was nice to be in the shelter and talking to a friendly voice.

'Joe,' I said eventually.

She chatted on for a while, not asking too many questions. 'If you've run away,' she said eventually, 'then there must be people who are concerned about you. And there are some nasty people out there at night who might hurt you.'

'No,' I said, suddenly vehement. 'I'm safe here. There's people already hurting me and doing fucking things to me.'

She didn't have to tell me about how many nasty people there were in the world, I'd met some of them personally, and I knew all too well it wasn't strangers hiding in the bushes at night who I had to be wary of; it was my own family and the people they introduced me to. I felt sure I knew more about the way the world worked than she did, for all her professional training and good intentions.

'Where are you from?' she asked, changing her tack, but I didn't tell her. Although she seemed very nice the conversation didn't seem to be going the way I had assumed and hoped it would. I don't know what I had expected to happen, but I hadn't been prepared to be bombarded with so many questions.

Then she told me she was having a problem with her phone.

'I'm just going to switch to another one,' she said. 'Hold on a second, Joe. Don't go away, I'll be right back.'

There was something about her voice that made me trust her so I hung on as she told me to. I thought about hanging up but then I would have had to go through the whole process again if I'd decided to ring back, so I stayed there, staring out into the blackness and the rain outside. She was gone for what seemed like ages but was probably only about half a minute. When she came back on the line she kept me talking for a bit longer about myself and what I should do, and then suddenly I was bathed in the unexpected glare of headlights, pinned down in the phone box like a cornered rabbit. Swinging round I saw the distinctive bonnet of a police car drawing up at the kerb outside. As the policeman climbed out of his car, pulling on his waterproofs, I realized it was the same man I had escaped from a few nights earlier down by the railway line. I knew I had to act fast because he wouldn't be taking any risks now he knew how desperate I was to get away. Dropping the phone I threw open the door and made a dash for it. This time, however, he was ready for me and grabbed my backpack as I went past, jerking me to a halt. I tried to wriggle free of the straps and extricate myself, but he got hold of my arm.

'Wo, calm down. Joe, calm down!' His voice wasn't as angry as I would have expected considering how I had messed him about the last time he'd caught me. He actually sounded quite friendly.

'Fuck off!' I shouted, struggling in vain to get free. 'I ain't going back! Fuck off! I ain't fucking going back to the bastards!'

At the time, I was convinced it had been the woman on the end of the helpline who had betrayed me. It's possible that the police car turned up by coincidence at that precise moment, but it seemed unlikely. What were the chances of him appearing out there in the middle of nowhere at that time of night at exactly the moment when I was on the line to her? Yet again I felt I had reached out to someone for help and been let down. I was so angry I exploded, thrashing and punching and kicking and shouting as he struggled to keep a grip on me.

'Stop fighting, Joe,' he said, trying to hold me at arm's length to protect himself. 'Please. I ain't gonna let you go this time so there's no point trying.'

Eventually I wore myself out. He was a lot stronger than me and I could tell he wasn't going to release me however hard I hit him. I resentfully allowed him to fold me into the back of his car, thinking I would let him think he had beaten me and wait for a better opportunity to get away. Once I was safely locked in the back he drove me to a tiny local police station nearby, which I think was probably just an office tacked onto the side of his house. At least it was warm and dry as we came in and he turned on the light. He locked the doors behind him and settled me down, making us both a cup of tea.

'Right,' he said, once I had calmed down and he felt he could talk to me rationally. 'We know who you are. You fit the description of a missing boy who's been reported as running away from home.'

'You can't fucking send me back there!' I started shouting again. 'And how did you fucking find me there in that fucking phone box anyway?'

'We knew you were there,' was all he said. 'We've been told that you claim you're being beaten by your mum. Is that true?'

I said nothing. I knew now that anything I did say would find its way back to her and she would kill me the moment she had the chance. I didn't want to make things any worse than they already were by accusing her of things that no one would ever believe were true anyway. It was beginning to look as though I had made a mistake by talking about it at all, so I decided to revert to not telling anyone anything.

'I'm not fucking going back there,' I muttered, desperately mustering all the bravado I could to hide the terror that was now overcoming my anger. 'You can't make me. I don't have to talk to you. You've got no right to keep me here.'

'Yes I have,' he corrected me patiently. 'Because you're a minor you need to be in protective custody.'

'I don't have to do anything you say, you prick!' I snarled, like a cornered dog fighting to the last, ready to bite any hand that was held out to me – literally, given my past history of attacking people.

'There's some officers coming from your local police station to pick you up,' he told me. 'They're the ones who have been investigating your disappearance.'

I felt a chill running through me. Would one of them be the man with the handcuffs? Or would they be friends of his? Would their report of whatever they had to say about me be read by him? Would he pass it on to Douglas, who would then report back to Amani and Mum? I stopped talking, hiding behind the mask of silence that had been my sanctuary for so many years, looking down at the floor as I had always been taught to. He left me in peace and an hour or two later the other officers turned up to collect me.

'This is Joe,' the first man told them. 'He's quite a handful, to say the least. Hang on to him tightly, he's got a habit of bolting.'

Not wanting to take any chances one of the new men pulled out a pair of handcuffs exactly like the ones I had worn so often when being raped by their colleague. He snapped them onto my wrist and attached me to himself, marching me out to the back of an unmarked car. Feeling the cold steel digging into my flesh brought back all my experiences with the policeman at Douglas's house, making me shake uncontrollably. It was as though I was being delivered back to them on a plate, as though they had reached out all this way and pulled me back into their web. It felt as if there would be nowhere I would ever be able to run to where they wouldn't be able to find me and bring me back. Now that I was in the police system, how long would it be before that policeman got to hear about my arrest and told Douglas and the rest where I was and what I had been saying? Anything I said now would be written down and recorded somewhere and they would know if I informed on them. God alone knew what they would do to me if that happened. All these panic-stricken thoughts were whirling round and round in my head as I sat in the back of the police car with one of my captors beside me and the other in the front, driving.

One copper tried to make a bit of small talk as we drove along, but I wasn't having any of it. I wasn't even sure that I would be able to force any words out past the stranglehold fear now had on my throat. It seemed that whenever people were nice to me it always ended badly. I had to keep my guard up, had to be watchful. Despite being brought back in like this, my short time on the run had emboldened me a little. I no longer felt that I was completely helpless. I actually did have choices as long as I wasn't trapped in a room with Mum or Amani or Douglas, and I could have some effect on what might happen to me if I stuck firmly enough to my guns and refused to make it easy for them to subdue me again.

'I swear to God,' I told him when I was finally calm enough to be able to stutter the words out, 'if you take me home I'll kill the fucking bitch.'

'That's not a very nice thing to say,' he said. 'Your mother is really concerned about you. She seems a very nice person.'

'A nice fucking person? You don't know fucking anything! She'll fucking beat me to death if you take me to her house. I swear I'll stick a knife in her if I have to go back.'

'Why are you talking like this? Your mum is worried and she wants you back.'

I could just imagine the performance she had been putting on for them, telling them what a difficult child I had been and what hell I had put her through, and how she had lost her beloved husband in a terrible accident and how I had done nothing but add to her troubles ever since. I'd heard her do it so many times before and the way I was behaving with the police now just confirmed to them everything she would have been saying about me being a problem child. Realizing that there was now a real danger I was going to be taken straight back home to the life I had walked out on a week or so before I went crazy again, like a wild animal trying to escape from a cage, determined to let them know just how desperate I was not to be returned to her.

'I ain't fucking going home!' I shouted. 'I ain't fucking going. She'll kill me!'

'Calm down, calm down,' the officer tried to restrain me in my seat as I thrashed wildly around. 'We're not taking you home, we're taking you back to the police station.'

'They'll hurt me again.'

'Who's going to hurt you?'

'My brother,' I blurted, still too frightened to mention Douglas and his friends.

'Why would your brother want to hurt you?'

'He keeps sticking his fucking willy up my bum!' I said, shocked to hear myself actually saying the words, embarrassed to admit to such a thing. No boy likes to confess to the fact that he has been raped, especially by his own brother – even if he knows it isn't his fault.

'You're definitely not going back home,' the copper assured me. 'Please calm down. You've got to trust us.'

'Why have you got me in these then,' I asked, pointing to the handcuffs, 'if you want me to trust you?'

'Okay,' he said after a moment's thought. 'I'm going to take them off so you can see I mean it.'

The doors were locked so there was no way I could get out anyway but it was a relief to feel them coming off, as if I was starting to win their trust. I tried to calm down and breathe a bit. I didn't want to make any bad mistakes; I wanted to be ready to jump at any opportunity to escape that might present itself. Even if they were starting to sound more understanding I still didn't trust them an inch and certainly didn't want to stay in any police station for a moment longer than I had to. I was terrified that I would come face to face with Uncle Douglas's friend and would then be totally at his mercy.

When we got to the police station nearest home I was escorted quickly into an interview room, allowing me no chance to do a runner. They sat me down with another cup of tea and a senior officer came in to join the one who had been in the back of the car with me. Their attitude certainly seemed to have changed, as they started to question me more gently about what had happened between my brother and me at home. It seemed that by talking about what he did to me I had set off some sort of procedural alarm bells and they were going to have to take the accusation seriously. Maybe it was occurring to them that there might be more reasons for my behaviour than they had been led to believe. For the first time ever, grown-up men in positions of authority actually seemed to be listening to me. I dare say they were feeling sorry for Mum too, imagining how devastated she would be to find out what her other son had been up to under her own roof, but I still didn't feel ready to try explaining her part in my nightmare of a life.

I didn't want to tell the officers any more details than I had to, but I wanted to say enough so that they would realize they couldn't let me go home, not even temporarily, while they undertook their enquiries. My brain was racing as I tried to work out the best way to protect myself. Larry had always been the ringleader of any abuse that he and Barry had inflicted on me, so I didn't bother to include Barry as well in my accusations. It was bad enough to admit that one brother had been raping me; another would have been even more humiliating and might even have started to make my story sound less credible. I don't know why I didn't tell them more about Mum and Amani and Uncle Douglas. I guess I still felt embarrassed to have to admit the extent of the abuse I had been subjected to, feeling dirty, humiliated, guilty and implicated myself in everything I had ever been forced to do over the years.

Although I was glad that they were finally paying attention and not just dismissing me as a hopeless troublemaker, I was now feeling nervous about having said too much. There is a certain amount of safety in being someone that no one takes any notice of. To suddenly find myself in the spotlight and the centre of attention was scary. I knew that when Mum got to hear about this she was definitely going to want to kill me and Larry would be in the queue right behind her. Now that I had made this accusation it was even more important that I made sure the police didn't send me back to the house.

'Can you give us more details?' they kept asking.

'No,' I said, my eyes constantly fixed on the floor. 'He just keeps interfering with me.'

Once they had heard me out they decided there was enough merit in the accusations for them to need to call in social services. I was pleased they were taking me seriously but nervous about having to deal with people who already knew all about my past record for being damaged. From the moment I had bitten the first welfare worker who came to the house to the moment I walked out of the school, they had a catalogue of evidence to show that I was an aggressive, disturbed boy. Would they think I was making up this whole story about Larry just to cause more problems for my family?

When the social worker arrived and they explained the situation to her I could see that she didn't believe a word I was saying but had to go through the motions.

'We've been to see your mum,' she told me and I could imagine just how convincing Mum would have been at that interview.

'She's told us that you have always been a disruptive influence in the family,' the social worker went on. 'She told me you've been causing trouble all your life.'

I stared at the floor and said nothing, knowing that if I said out loud some of the things that were going through my head I would simply be confirming her prejudices. When they went back through the files they found all the reports of me being traumatized by Dad's death, and now the police had heard me ranting and raving and swearing about how I was going to kill Mum if they sent me home, so it was looking to them as if Mum was right and I was the problem. Perhaps they would have looked further into the causes of all my disruptive behaviour if they hadn't been able to see a perfect explanation in Dad's death. What they all saw when they looked at me was an aggressive troublemaker who distracted other children in school and gave his poor family endless heartache. My only hope was that they would believe what I said about Larry, or at least decide that it was enough of a possibility for them not to be able to take the risk of sending me back.

'Because of the seriousness of your allegation against your brother,' they eventually told me, 'you need to go to a care home while we do some investigating.'

To my relief they sent me to a holding and assessment unit where they kept children until they worked out what best to do with us regarding homes, fostering, adoption, education and all the other options. It was a mansion of a place, very clinical, cold and daunting, and felt more like a prison than a children's home. One side of the building was used for social services offices and there were a lot of cameras tracking our movements, so there wasn't exactly a trusting atmosphere. The system was strict, although fair. They genuinely did seem to want to find a way of saving me from myself, but I couldn't bring myself to trust them and was proving to be a challenge to their patience.

Although I continued to be difficult, I did feel that at least the policeman had kept his word about not sending me home and I thought maybe there was some hope that once they had completed their investigations they would believe me and let me stay away from Mum and the rest of them until I was old enough to live on my own.

The day after I arrived at the home the same policeman who had brought me back in the car came to see me.

'We've arrested your brother,' he said, and I felt my heart lift. If Larry had confessed then I was willing to tell them everything, even about Uncle Douglas and his friends, including the policeman with the handcuffs. 'And he's denied everything. Your mum says you're a liar. We've spoken to your school and they've confirmed you're disruptive too.'

My hopes plummeted as quickly as they had soared. It was just as I should have expected – I wasn't going to be believed. I didn't say anything, just stared at the floor and waited to learn what my fate was going to be.

'Your mum is so fed up with you she says she doesn't want you back. She's at the end of her tether.'

Suddenly there was hope again, even though they had returned to preferring to believe that I was the problem, not Mum and Larry. It might have been for the wrong reasons, but at least I had managed to get out of the house and free of Mum's iron grip. Everyone might have decided I was a liar and a bad boy, but at least I wouldn't be getting any more beatings or abuse for a while. I guess Mum must have been panicking after the visits from the police. As long as I was mute or too terrified to speak to anyone she had felt safe, but I had finally found the courage to use my voice and even though I hadn't been believed this time, there was still a possibility she was in danger of being uncovered. Now that I had dared to speak to a policeman she would never be able to rely on keeping me quiet in the future. That, I assume, was why she had announced she didn't want me back in her house.

We slept in dormitories at the children's home, with screens between the beds, and the staff were constantly checking on us through the night. It wasn't a comfortable place to be, but I still felt safer than I had ever felt at home. At least no one was going to attack me there, or make me do anything I didn't want to do. The worst part of it was the boredom as we sat around watching television or playing pool – but then I was used to that from the many hours I had been left on my own at home either in my darkened cell or in a bedroom where I was forbidden to move or do anything.

Most of the staff's time at the home was spent assessing and interviewing us all individually, so there was nothing for the rest of us to do whenever it was someone else's turn to go into the office. None of the staff had any time for joking with us or even for getting to know us better; they just had to get on with their duties of care. In that respect they were more like prison officers than social workers. I think if there had been anyone available to sit down with me and win my trust at that stage I would have been ready to start talking about the things that had happened to me, but I was suspicious of everyone, having been betrayed so many times, and none of them had the time to help me overcome those suspicions.

Most of the other children in the home came and went quite quickly, but I was one of the more difficult and challenging cases and it seemed to be giving them a problem working out what to do with me. I was constantly anxious about what their ultimate decision would be, terrified that Mum would change her mind and say she'd have me back and they would decide to send me home just because they couldn't think what else to do with me.

Once the assessment process had been completed, they told me, they would either send me home or on to another care home for a longer stay, or to foster parents. Who, I wondered, would want to foster a foulmouthed teenage boy who saw the whole world as being against him and had a reputation for being disruptive and for running away? And, if someone did foster me, who was to say they wouldn't abuse me in just the same way everyone else had? Staying in the care system seemed like my best bet. All I could do was wait and hope and see what was decided by people I didn't even know. It is a scary feeling to have virtually no power to influence anything that happens in your own life.

Chapter Fifteen

In and out of Care

Once I had been accepted into the care system I was moved back and forth between a number of homes for a few weeks as they tried to work out the best thing to do with me. I know that I was a right handful to any staff who tried to help me. I was so angry at the world and so suspicious of all the people in it that I wasn't willing to give anyone the benefit of the doubt. Anyone who had shown me any kindness in the past had ended up letting me down: Dad by dying, Wally and Pete by leaving, Douglas by tricking me into liking him with handfuls of sweets, John and possibly even the helpline lady for turning me over to the police. I didn't trust any of the key workers who professed to have my best interests at heart. I decided it was better to keep them all at arm's length if I wanted to avoid being hurt all over again. So I did whatever I liked and treated everyone like shit, fulfilling Mum's description of me perfectly. I was a nightmare and it wasn't long before they were all looking for a way to pass the problem on to someone else. I was too much trouble for anyone to want to cope with me.

About a month after I was picked up from the phone box, the worst thing possible happened and someone managed to persuade Mum to take me back home. Maybe they thought they were doing me a favour by talking my mother into trying again with me. I don't know what changed her mind. Perhaps she had thought about it and decided it would be safer to keep me close so she would know what I was saying to people. Or maybe she was missing the money that I brought in to her from Uncle Douglas. When they told me what had been decided I went just as crazy as I had in the back of the police car a month earlier. There was no way I was going to go back peacefully, but this time they weren't taking any notice. As far as they were concerned I was a pain in the neck and they believed I had even made up false allegations about my brother in order to try to get my own way. They wanted rid of me as soon as possible, so three staff at the care home restrained me, bundled me into the back of a white van and drove me to Mum's house, fighting and screaming all the way. I felt there was nothing in the world I could do or say to convince them that they were making a mistake, that they were delivering me back to the devil herself, transporting me to my execution. It was just like being in one of my nightmares as I dreamed I was struggling to get out of the front door but was being dragged backwards. It didn't matter how much I struggled in that van, it still kept on driving towards Mum's house. I might just as well have been mute again for all the notice the key workers were taking of my pleading and shouting.

When they dropped me off at the house, holding onto me so tightly as we approached the front door that I couldn't possibly run, or even move, Mum was at her most charming, welcoming her prodigal son back home, making me look even more like a vile, ungrateful brat to the care home staff. The moment they had left the house and the front door had closed behind them the smile vanished from her face and the temper I had been expecting erupted from deep inside her.

'Get in there,' she commanded, grabbing my hair and dragging me into the second lounge, where all the curtains were tightly drawn as always, and I knew I was doomed. Amani appeared from nowhere the moment he heard the care workers drive off in their van and together they gave me the hiding of my life. For the first time ever I tried to fight back, refusing to lie down and accept it any more, but that only stoked up their fury to even more terrible heights. They were both far bigger and stronger than me and together they were invincible.

Amani used his belt and once I was down on the floor they were both kicking and punching and whipping with all their strength, throwing me round the room like a rag doll, smacking my head against the walls as hard as they could. It felt as though they were actually trying to kill me.

'What did you tell those fucking coppers, you little bastard?' Amani was yelling, obviously fearful he would lose his lucrative connections with Uncle Douglas and his friends, but I didn't have enough breath in my body to be able to put his mind at rest and tell him that I had said nothing.

'I told you I'd fucking kill you if you ever breathed a word about what went on in this family to anyone,' Mum screamed as she landed kick after kick on my prone body.

The blows were so hard they made me retch and vomit. Once she and Amani had exhausted themselves and I was lying on the floor in a crumpled heap, Mum called Larry and Barry in and ordered them to watch me. They then ripped my clothes off and did what they wanted to me and I was too weak and defeated to put up any struggle.

'I'll fucking give you something to tell the police,' Larry said through gritted teeth as he set to work.

By the time they had finished I was so bruised and battered there was no way I could get to school the following day without somebody noticing the damage they'd inflicted, so they kept me off for a week, ringing in to say I was ill. As far as I am aware, no one from the social services came to check up that the handover had gone all right. No one from the school came to check that I really was ill. They obviously hadn't believed a word I had said and had been completely convinced by Mum's performance. Or maybe they had decided our whole family was a lost cause and too much trouble to deal with.

All through the following week one or other of them was with me every minute of the day to make sure I didn't make another bid for freedom or get hold of any sort of implement I could use to defend myself. They beat me and raped me whenever the urge took them. But even Mum knew that they couldn't keep me imprisoned in the house for ever now that the outside world was aware of my existence and after a week, when the most visible of my wounds had healed, they had to let me go back to school if they didn't want to risk receiving another visit from the authorities. All through the Sunday before I went back she warned me and threatened me with what would happen if I breathed so much as another word about anything to anyone. She went on and on, shouting and yelling, making my head spin. In the end she pressed a knife against my neck.

'I'm fucking telling you,' she screamed, 'next time I will kill you!' And I believed her.

She escorted me all the way to the school gates on the Monday morning and I didn't say a word, just staring straight ahead of me, waiting for my chance. The moment I knew she was off the school premises I walked out again into the lane that ran down the back of the building, not even bothering to change out of my uniform this time. Now I knew that it was possible to just walk away I wasn't going to stay around for a moment longer than I had to. They were beating me anyway, so what did I have to lose by trying to get away?

I didn't have any plan this time, in fact I was still in a bit of a daze, but I set off back in the same direction I had gone in before. This time I hadn't walked for more than an hour before a police car drew up ahead of me and a policeman got out of the passenger door, pulling his cap on as he walked back towards me. I thought about making a run for it, but I was too tired and I thought he would almost certainly be able to catch me so I just stood there and waited for him to get to me.

'What are you doing, sonny?' he asked.

He held me firmly while his driver did a radio check, which told him that I had gone missing from the school.

'Come on lad,' he said. 'Back to school.'

They took me in to see the headmaster when we got there and he asked me what was going on and why I was behaving the way I was.

'I'm not going back home,' I told him, not looking up from the floor.

'Why not?' he asked.

'Because they're hurting me again,' I said, unable to find any other way of explaining it.

'What can I do to keep you in school, Joe?' he asked.

He was a decent, old-fashioned sort of teacher and he knew that because of my learning difficulties it was even more important than normal that I had some sort of education for as long as possible. I appreciated his well-meaning concern but I knew he didn't actually have a clue what my life was really like. How could anyone imagine it who hadn't been through something similar? I just shrugged, not having any answer for him. He sighed and the usual procedures were set in motion. A social worker was called in to deal with me, yet another person taking me aside and trying to persuade me to explain what was going on in my head. Once again I told them that if they sent me home I would smash the place up, 'and I'll hurt her this time,' I promised. 'I'll really hurt her.'

It was just boyish bravado because even though I was growing up – almost fourteen now – Mum was still ten times stronger than me when she was angry. If I had been able to get my hands on any sort of sharp implement I would have stabbed her at that stage, I'm sure of it. The social workers must have been starting to worry about the risk I would do something really bad, given how aggressively I was behaving. They weren't to know that I was watched every second that I was in the house and never allowed near the kitchen or anywhere else where I might be able to find a weapon to use in my own defence, or to launch an attack.

'We've contacted your mother,' the social worker continued, regardless.

'If she shows up here I'll fucking kill her,' I shouted.

It was as though I was talking to myself. No one was taking any notice at all. I sometimes wondered what the point had been in teaching me how to speak if no one was willing to listen to anything I had to say. Mum arrived in the headmaster's office to take me home as if the whole incident had just been another minor infringement of the school rules, and the moment she walked in I completely lost all control. I didn't care any more if she heard what I had to say about her. She was going to kill me anyway if she got her hands on me. I was no longer willing to sit with my eyes on the floor, unable to speak up for myself.

'Come on, Joe,' she said in her most reasonable voice, and I started to rage around the office, sweeping everything off the headmaster's desk, smashing up the room like a madman.

'This is what he's always like,' she said, standing back and allowing me to prove every bad thing she had ever told anyone about me. They must all have felt so sorry for her, believing her to be a decent woman trying to do her best by her delinquent, ungrateful son.

'Ah, fuck him,' she said eventually, as if her saintly patience had finally snapped. 'I've had enough. I don't want him back.'

Once she said that there was nothing the social workers could do to dissuade her and they took me back into care, into a home that I actually quite liked, despite my destructive behaviour and resentful attitude. I felt safe there, the food was good and no one bothered me. I didn't see Mum or the rest of the family again for six months. It seemed there was a chance I had managed to escape at last.

Over the next two years I would meet a lot of different care workers in a variety of homes. Now and again I would come across someone who truly seemed to want to help the kids in their care to live better lives, someone who would spend time talking to us, listening to us, organizing things for us to do. The vast majority, however, were obviously looking to do as little as possible in order to earn their wages. They would spend most of their time in the staff room, drinking tea, only coming out if there was trouble that needed sorting out. They would become impatient with any interruptions to their privacy, telling us to go away if we ever dared to knock on their door for some reason they considered trivial. I know we were probably difficult to handle, me more than most, but the majority of them certainly didn't do anything to improve the situations that we provoked.

They were always quite good about giving us our pocket money if we needed to buy clothes, or even just to go to the cinema, as long as they were within their weekly budgets. They were happy to see us get out from under their feet for a while and I guess it saved them the trouble of organizing anything for us themselves. At one home they had a sixteen-seater minibus but I don't remember any of us ever going out in it, although it was occasionally used to take one or other of us to the doctor or the hospital. Of course we didn't always spend the pocket money they gave us on whatever we said we were going to, and usually we would end up hanging around outside off-licences asking grown-ups to buy drink and cigarettes for us. It's amazing how many of them would agree to it and I was often drunk when I got back to the homes, but the staff hardly ever noticed. When I was out and about I always wore shiny shell suits, trainers and a baseball cap, like it was some sort of uniform, the peak of the cap pulled down low over my eyes to hide them from the disapproving or wary looks of passers-by.

At one stage the authorities moved me to a smaller children's home in a converted council house, which was run more along the lines of a family home. I guess they were hoping to make me socialize a bit more normally. It was still run by social workers but there were some younger kids there as well as older ones. There was a lad in the house called Ben, who was ten, and we used to get up to a lot of mischief together. One night we went down to raid the pantry after everyone had gone to bed. I pushed against the glass door to open it and must have put too much force into it because my hand went straight through and was badly sliced. They had to rush me to hospital and stitch me up, leaving yet another scar that I still carry to this day.

There was a girl in the home called Jean who was a bit behind mentally, even more than I was. She was a year or so older than me and she let it be known that she fancied me. Although I was fed up with being made to have sex with men and boys I had always liked having sex with girls. I wanted to be normal and I didn't want to think of myself as being gay, as I believed Larry and Barry were, so I wasn't completely disinterested in her advances, even though I didn't fancy her much.

I was in the bathroom in my underpants one day, running a bath, when Jean walked straight in and locked the door behind her. Even though she wasn't exactly attractive, when she started touching me inappropriately my body responded as most adolescent boys' bodies would under the circumstances, especially a boy who had been forced into as much sexual activity as I had by that time. Realizing my luck was in I followed my instincts and we ended up having sex on the bathroom floor. Because it was a relatively small house everyone always knew what was going on and within minutes other kids were outside the door shouting encouragement. Ben was sex mad and he was the main one egging me on and asking for details of what was happening. With the benefit of hindsight I guess something must have happened to him to make him so fruity so young, but we never talked about those sorts of things. The noise soon brought the staff running upstairs and hammering on the door, demanding that we stop what we were doing and come out.

Although I was a bit embarrassed by the fuss I didn't think I had done anything particularly wrong. Due to my past I saw nothing unusual in having sexual intercourse if it was mutually consensual but, not surprisingly, the social workers were horrified when they realized what had happened under their care and immediately held a conference about the problem. It's hard to imagine how many hours must have been spent over the years by people discussing what they should do with me, even though they didn't really know anything about what was going on in my life or in my head.

Because Jean was a good bit more backward than me they saw me as the culprit and accused me of taking advantage of her, although it was her who had come on to me first and the whole thing had been mutual. I suppose, technically speaking, I had 'taken advantage', although I had not forced her to do anything. What I had done wasn't right, but it was hardly surprising that I was confused about right and wrong at that time and Jean certainly never did anything she didn't want to do.

With all the normal resentments of a teenager in care, I felt as though I was being picked on and I got so fed up with one particular social worker who was making out I was some sort of sex maniac that I eventually lost my temper. I stormed out to the car park and turned over his little 2CV car, rolling it right over onto its roof. It was as if my temper had given me superhuman strength, just as Mum's always did.

If the social workers thought I was so sexually mixed-up and precocious, I wonder now why didn't they try to find out how I had got to be that way? Looking back I can't understand why it didn't all click into place for them, but they continued to follow Mum's line that I was disturbed and difficult because of Dad's death and that was the end of the story. Rolling a social worker's car over did nothing but illustrate exactly what she was telling them.

As a result of my relationship with Jean I was moved back to the bigger children's home and another blot was added to my record. I must have been beginning to look like a bit of a hopeless case to those who were still trying to find a way to help me. No one even came close to winning my trust and getting me to tell them what had made me the way I was.

Chapter Sixteen

Thieving for Mum

After six months of me living in the care homes, Mum came back into my life, being all nice again and asking me to go home. When they told me she wanted to see me I felt an immediate surge of fear, even though I knew she couldn't actually attack me when there were other people around. Although I didn't want to see her I was told I had no choice and there was a tiny part of me that looked forward to hearing how Thomas was getting on. However terrible my family life had been, it was still my family and there was an emotional tie that even she hadn't been able to obliterate totally. When she arrived at the home I discovered she was pregnant with Amani's baby, which would be her seventh in all. It made me feel sick to think that yet another kid was going to be brought into the world to be placed at her mercy.

'I promise nothing will happen to you if you come back now,' she assured me with all the sincerity she was capable of. 'And I'll keep the boys away from you.'

I didn't believe her for a second and she must have been able to see that. It's hard to imagine how she found the nerve to even think of asking, knowing how often she had betrayed me in the past, but my mother never lacked nerve. She seemed to be blaming it all on Larry and Barry now, when they were only ever doing what she told them or gave them permission to do.

'Look,' she said, her face a picture of reasonableness, 'I know I've done wrong by you in the past and I'm really sorry for everything.'

I just stood with my arms folded, listening.

'Amani's gone now,' she said, as if he had been the one who was the problem, not her. 'I've got rid of him.'

That made me feel a bit better, because I knew I stood a better chance of being able to protect myself from one of her tempers if it was just her I was fighting against. I had never stood a chance against the two of them – no one did. I still couldn't really work out why she wanted me back when she had spent so many years telling me how much she hated me and wanted to kill me. Maybe, I thought, it was because Amani wasn't there and she liked having the house full of people who would do what she told them.

Despite all she had done to me, and even though I still didn't trust her not to turn on me again, I decided to give her a chance. There must be something so instinctive inside us when we are thinking about our mothers, something that makes us want to believe they love us despite any evidence to the contrary. Why else would I even have considered going back to live with someone who had hated me so vehemently and had so deliberately set out to hurt me and exploit me for years on end? I wanted to believe I had a mummy who loved me, even if it had to be this woman. I wanted her to be the same with me as she was with Ellie, and with Larry and Barry. I tried to convince myself that she was finally telling the truth and that things would be different now that I was older and more able to look after myself, that I would be accepted as part of the family rather than looked on as the dirty little bastard who had to go under the table and be fed on scraps like a dog.

Perhaps one of the main reasons I went back was that I felt more confident from the months of being away and all the experiences I'd had in that time. I also felt safer because I knew that if things got bad again at least I could walk out and come back to the care home. I believed I had more control over my own life now that I was almost fifteen – nearly an adult – and I was fairly sure that no one would be able to do the things they had done to me in the past. I also wanted to see my little brother

Thomas again, who I had always liked and who had been through a lot of the same stuff I had, although neither of us had ever really talked about it frankly.

By this stage, the council had moved Mum to a smaller, more modern property. It was semi-detached again but was only on two floors and located in a different area of the city. It was a nice house with a big garden at the back. Mum was beginning to get arthritis in her legs and all the stairs and the cleaning at the old house had started to give her problems. It was hard to imagine that someone who had been such a terrifying force of nature might actually be growing older and more vulnerable. I noticed that she was beginning to look more like an old woman than I remembered, wearing old-fashioned clothes like bedroom slippers and baggy black trousers all day and every day around the house. When she went down the pub she would still dress up in bright floral dresses, but she had put on weight and they were starting to look alarming on a woman of her size. She would still always make an effort with her appearance when she went out, her hair and make-up immaculate, but she no longer looked young.

That didn't stop men from picking her up in the pub once Amani had gone from the scene, although I dare say they had mostly had a few drinks by the time they actually decided to go home with her. She used to take them straight up to her bedroom and we could often hear them going at it. We would all try to stay out of the way but occasionally we would see the men sneaking out in the morning and some of them were about as rough as it's possible to imagine. I think she would get so drunk at night she lost all sense of judgement about those sorts of things. But then Amani hadn't been any sort of oil painting, so maybe looks didn't matter to her.

When I agreed to come back home she said that I could share a bedroom with Ellie and Thomas, separating me from Larry and Barry just as she had promised. That seemed a good start. It turned out to be true that Amani had gone, and so had all trace of Uncle Douglas and his other seedy friends. As far as I could tell Amani had gone back to my Aunt Melissa and his relationship with Mum had just dissolved. The others told me that she had tried to get some commitment from him when she found she was pregnant by him but he had felt like she was trying to trap him so he had walked away. I don't think he even came around for the birth of the new baby. I certainly never saw him again.

Mum did seem to be trying really hard to overcome the nasty side of her personality and often apologized to us for the mistakes she had made in the past at moments when she was feeling sorry for herself – particularly when she'd had a few too many drinks. I tried to suppress all the memories that I carried, wanting to start again and not to be reminded about any of it, but it was hard sometimes. The fact that we were living in a different house helped because it meant I didn't have to be in the same rooms where I had been imprisoned and tortured, helping to avoid the stirring up of my blackest thoughts.

To begin with I allowed myself to believe that she actually meant what she was saying and that she was genuinely sorry for everything she had done, but then it dawned on me that the real reason she wanted me back was to have another potential breadwinner in the house. Over the years I worked as a 'porn star' she had been funding her drinking from the money that Amani was bringing in from Uncle Douglas and the rest, but now that had gone she was broke. She needed to get as many of her children working as she could, and persuade them to hand over their earnings to her, in order to keep enough cash coming in.

The first week that I was home went quite well as she tried to lull me into a sense of security, then in the second week she started talking about how she wanted me, Thomas and Ellie to start earning our keep. I was immediately on my guard, fearful of what she might have planned for us and ready to make a run for it the moment anyone like Douglas showed up at the door. Larry and Barry were too bone idle to do anything and she didn't seem to think she could force them any more now they were in their mid twenties, so she kept up the pressure on us, suggesting things we could do. I was shocked by how normal, honest and sensible the suggestions seemed to begin with.

She started by sending us out to wash people's cars, knocking on doors and charging a pound a car. We got really keen and were doing twenty or thirty cars a day quite quickly, excited by the amount of money we managed to fill our pockets with by the end of a hard day's work. The moment we got home, of course, she would take the money straight off us and head down the pub with it. We were really working hard and I began to resent losing the money so quickly, particularly when she wasn't using it to buy anything for any of us.

'Why am I giving you everything I earn?' I asked one day, having been lulled into a false sense of security by her apparent change of character. 'I don't mind giving you a bit, but we should be allowed to keep some of what we earn.'

The moment the words were out of my mouth I realized my mistake because her fist punched hard into my face, sending me spinning across the room. All the memories came erupting back to the surface as I tried to pull myself together and clear my head. They threatened to overwhelm me and for a second I was going to retaliate with any weapon I could find. But something stopped me. I don't know if it was because I feared I would make her even angrier, or if I was actually able to rationalize the situation and realized I would only make my own situation worse. Instead of hitting her back, I walked straight out of the house and returned to the care home, telling them that Mum had assaulted me again. They could see the bruise deepening on my face, making my eye swell until it was almost closed, but when they went round to see her she made up a long story about how I had been being disruptive and smashing up the house and that she had had to restrain me. To my horror they believed her yet again.

I admit that my behaviour over the previous months in the homes had not done anything to help my reputation so it was probably easier than it should have been for the authorities to accept that I was just up to my old tricks again. As far as they were concerned, my mother had done her best to put me on the straight and narrow, only to be met by ingratitude and violence. I stayed at the care home anyway because I refused to go back and I was getting a bit too big to be easily forced to do anything I didn't want to do.

A month later Mum came round again trying to persuade me to return home for another attempt at reconciliation. For the whole year that I was fifteen, I kept going back and forth, each time hoping that it would be different and each time being disappointed. Her mood swings were even more unpredictable than they had been before. Whereas when I was small she was always angry and always aggressive towards me, she now had moments when she was all sweetness and light, but it was impossible to predict when those moments would disappear and she would be back to screaming and punching and dragging me or Thomas around by our hair. Despite her arthritis she was still a formidable force when she was angry and something stopped me from fighting back with all my strength. Despite all the threats I had issued over the years, I always held back from actually hitting my own mother, which meant she still had the power to rule over me as long as I was in her house.

As soon as her mood blackened Larry and Barry would appear at her side to assist her in whatever beating she was administering, just as they always had, like two evil henchmen, never wanting to miss out on any possible blood-letting. Still I kept hoping that she would eventually stop picking on me and would start treating me the same way she treated them. I kept on giving her one more chance, despite the endless disappointments. Larry and Barry were both very hard men by that time and even she wouldn't have tried taking them on beyond the occasional passing clip round the ear to remind them who was the ultimate boss.

At least I had the freedom to come and go from the house as and when I wanted, and to make friends wherever I chose. At one stage I got to know an old boy called

McDermott, who used to run a little garage down the road, a bit like the one Dad had worked in. He must have felt sorry for me or something because he spent a lot of time chatting to me and letting me help him with odd jobs, giving me the occasional pound here and there or buying me a McDonalds for my lunch. Once I felt completely comfortable with him I would accept invitations to go back to his house for lunch, which was always really nice and companionable. I felt he was treating me as a fellow adult. In reality he was probably trying to keep me occupied and out of trouble, but if so then that was kind of him too. He would be happy to let me talk about Dad all the time, something I still wanted to do, just like when I was younger and kept obsessively drawing pictures of him on fire. There weren't many people who I could do that with because I would never have dared to mention Dad's name at home for fear of the repercussions.

One day McDermott and I dropped in to visit a mate of his on the way back from our lunch and I needed to use the toilet so I popped up to the bathroom. While I was in there I spotted a gold sovereign ring lying on the side of the basin and slipped it into my pocket. It was such a stupid thing to do, more of a habit than anything else because Mum was always encouraging us to nick anything we could. I would never have taken anything from McDermott himself because he was my friend, but this seemed like fair game because it was a stranger's house. The plan in our house was always to try to turn everything into money so a couple of days later I went down to a jeweller's in town and asked them to buy the ring. The jeweller took it from me and examined it carefully.

'This is stolen,' he said without giving it back. 'I'm not buying this.'

'No it's not,' I lied. 'It's my dad's and he's passed it on to me.'

'It's not your dad's.' He was obviously completely confident and wasn't taking any notice of anything I was saying. 'It's stolen.'

He wouldn't give it back to me and I realized then that McDermott must have been into the local shops to tip them off and ask them to keep an eye out for the ring, assuming I would be in with it sooner or later. Looking up, I saw that the shop was fitted with a CCTV camera so I knew there was no way I would be able to deny that it was me who had brought the ring in. McDermott would know for sure that I had stolen his mate's property. I felt so ashamed and angry with myself.

Sure enough, McDermott turned up on the doorstep at our house the next day to tell me how disappointed he was. He said they weren't calling the police but that I wasn't to come round to the garage again. I was as bitterly disappointed with my behaviour as he was. He had been the first adult who had taken the time to be my friend without being paid by the social services, the first to treat me decently without wanting something from me in return and I'd messed it up by betraying him. As usual Mum gave me a beating for being stupid enough to get caught, but I felt I deserved it anyway for being so treacherous towards McDermott and so careless of his friendship. Yet again I had proved that Mum was right and I was a bad lot. I still feel guilty about stealing that ring, even to this day.

It is hard to shake off the conditioning of years. Mum had always encouraged us to take whatever we could and as we got older she would send us out on any number of organized scams. Back when I was fourteen, for instance, she had decided the whole family should become regular churchgoers. She had grown friendly with a local vicar, who she'd met in the pub. She told Thomas and me that we were to go and help him to look after the Sunday school kids and take the collections in church during the services.

'If you can,' she told us, 'put your hand into the collections and stick some money into your pocket. Try to get as much as you can.'

Her request didn't seem anything out of the ordinary to us, it was just the way things were. That didn't mean, however, that we weren't scared of getting caught, knowing that she would give us a good battering if we were. For the first couple of weeks we were far too frightened to do anything, but she kept on and on at us and in the end we gave in, shoving handfuls of money down our underpants when the vicar wasn't looking, shocked to find how easily we got away with it. Regular members of the congregation used to put in envelopes with their name and their donations written on the outside and cash on the inside, so we knew which were the big ones. Some of them used to give up to forty pounds at a time. Opening them when we got home was like celebrating Christmas every week. To give us more incentive, Mum finally agreed to give us a cut of the takings rather than keeping it all for herself and to our shame we fell for it. We got greedier and greedier every time we got away with it, pushing more and more of the envelopes into our underpants every week.

After a year or so, the vicar noticed that his takings were badly down and worked out that we were by far the most likely source of the shortfall. One Sunday there was a different vicar conducting the service, but Thomas and I didn't take much notice until the usual one appeared behind us, tapped us both on the shoulder after the collection had been taken and asked us to step outside halfway through the visiting priest's sermon. It turned out they had been watching us without us realizing and had seen every move we'd made. Thomas had chickened out that week so I had nicked his share as well, and I hadn't even bothered to push it into my underpants. I'd grown so cocky about the whole operation I'd just stuffed the booty into my pocket.

'We know that money has been going missing,' the vicar told us once he got us outside. His voice was calm but firm, as if he was very sure of his facts.

'What you trying to say, you prick?' I demanded while Thomas was stuttering and stammering around in a blind panic

'I want you to empty your pockets,' the vicar continued patiently, choosing to ignore my aggression.

'You've no right to search us,' I said, climbing up onto my high horse.

'In that case,' he said quietly, 'I'm calling the police.'

'Have you seen us stealing anything?' I challenged him.

'No, but we know a number of our members' donations have been going missing.'

'Maybe it was the church clerk who nicked them,' I suggested.

'No, Joe, it wasn't.'

I kept arguing for as long as I could, desperately hoping something would occur to me before I had to empty my pockets and be exposed.

'Empty your pockets,' I commanded Thomas, my voice brimming with righteous indignation at being so falsely accused. 'Just to show him you've got nothing.'

In the split second that the vicar was distracted by Thomas's movements I transferred the envelopes from my pocket to my underpants, almost castrating myself on the sharp edges in the process. Once he had seen that Thomas had nothing he turned to me.

'Nothing in my pockets,' I said cheerfully, turning them inside out and praying none of the envelopes would work their way down my trouser leg while I was still standing in front of him.

'Fair enough, lads,' he said, nodding for us to go. I could see he knew what was going on but had decided not to pursue it any further just then. As I walked gingerly away I must have looked as though I'd had an accident in my pants. When I got home I told Mum that we were going to have to pack the scam in because the vicar was onto us, which did not please her.

That evening he came knocking and told Mum that he didn't want Thomas or me in his church any more.

'Why?' she asked, her eyes wide with innocence, as if this was the first she'd heard of any problem. 'What have they done?'

'They've been stealing money from the collections,' he told her gently, as if worried about shocking the poor, dear woman with such shameful news about her own children.

She gave a wonderful performance, saying she couldn't believe what she was hearing and clipped us round the ear in front of him, despite us squealing our innocence and accusing the church clerk of being the culprit. The vicar seemed satisfied that justice had been done.

'Thank you for sorting them out,' he said. 'Obviously you are welcome in the church any time, but not them.'

Mum didn't bother with the church any more after that and Thomas and I got another beating for being greedy and taking too much money.

'But you've been spending it!' I protested, my courage growing a little more with each confrontation, but she didn't want to hear anything from me – she just wanted to vent her anger at losing such a good source of income.

I went back to the care home the following day, nursing my latest bruises, but then she came round to apologize and promise yet another fresh start if I came home. So yet again I allowed her to sway me and went back.

She moved on from sending us to church to sending us on shoplifting expeditions, giving us very specific instructions about what to get for her. Clothing was a favourite and she would tell us exactly what sizes to go for. Thomas and I became expert shoplifters, stuffing things into our rucksacks that she could sell down the pub later the same day. We would steal pots and pans or toys or anything she wanted. She soon realized that she could turn a better profit from flogging our ill-gotten gains than she could from our car-washing business and she became more and more ambitious in her demands.

Thomas and I were walking past a bike shop with her one time and she nodded towards some bikes that were on display outside.

'I want them,' she said. 'All four of them.'

I couldn't see how Thomas and I were going to get away with two each so we had to recruit a couple of friends and persuade them it would be a lark. We plucked up our courage while we were out of sight and then made a run for it, grabbing the bikes from their stands and riding off, laughing as the irate shopkeeper shouted after us. I never liked stealing, but it was better than being beaten by Mum and it always set the adrenaline rushing. Apart from wanting to avoid a beating for disobeying her orders, I wanted to do things to please her, to win her love, to try to prove that just because I was Dad's favourite she didn't have to hate me forever. I was her son too and I was willing to do whatever she asked within reason to gain her love.

I only ever got caught shoplifting once, in Woolworths. I was with Thomas but he had managed to get away before I was grabbed. I was terrified when the store detective who had caught me said he was going to ring Mum. That was a much more frightening prospect than having to deal with the police. I pleaded for mercy but it had no effect and in the end the store manager called both the police and Mum. Yet again I was trapped in a room with my eyes on the floor, unable to say anything in my defence because Mum was standing right beside me, listening to every word. The police asked the manager if he wanted to press charges.

'No,' he said. 'I'm happy to leave it at that because his mother seems quite strict.'

'Oh, believe me,' Mum said, 'I'm going to sort him out when I get him home. He won't be doing anything like this again.'

The store manager seemed satisfied as he watched me being literally dragged out of his office by my ear. Once we were safely in the house I was given another beating for being so useless. I then headed back to the care home for sanctuary, telling them that I didn't want to stay at home any longer. It sometimes felt as though I was trapped in a cycle that would never be broken – in care, back at Mum's, in care again. At least I had choices, though, and that made me feel a lot stronger than I ever had before.

Chapter Seventeen

Moving On

Thomas and I got closer over that year. I was fifteen and he was almost thirteen by then and my best mate in the world as well as being my baby brother. I knew he had been through many of the same ordeals as me and that gave us a bond I didn't share with anyone else. At weekends when I was at home, if we had any spare time, he and I would go scrumping apples in next door's garden, which drove our neighbour mad. Or we would go over to the woods behind our house just to get away and talk about our lives and our plans for what we would do the moment we were old enough to escape Mum once and for all. The neighbours tried complaining to Mum once or twice about us stealing from their garden and she actually used to stick up for us, which meant she fell out with them just as surely as she had fallen out with poor old Paddy at the previous house.

Larry and Barry remained unbearable, though. I never had any kind of decent relationship with either of them. One day I went for a wander in the woods on my own and, as I trampled through the undergrowth, I suddenly came across Barry lying naked on his back with his legs in the air and Larry on top of him. My stomach turned over at the sight.

'Get off him!' I shouted, giving Larry a shove.

Larry grabbed hold of my arm tightly. 'You've got no right to fucking say anything, and if you do you'll get a battering!'

They carried on with what they had been doing, and it made me want to retch. It brought back so many disgusting memories that I had suppressed of what happened at Uncle Douglas's house: twosomes, threesomes, the men who just liked to watch, and that older lad who'd enjoyed it all and explained to the rest of us how to do it right. How could Barry be getting pleasure from something I had found such torture? But then, he was twenty-four now and I'd only been nine when it started.

'Fuck off, you little wanker!' Barry shouted.

I walked away feeling angry and confused. Once my eyes had been opened to it I realised it was happening all the time and the two of them were constantly disappearing off into the woods together. They tried to convince me that it was all just a bit of fun and that I should join in with them but I couldn't get my head round it. I'd been in the outside world enough to realise that it wasn't normal behaviour for brothers to have sex with each other. It was sick and wrong and I didn't want to be anywhere near it.

I found it increasingly difficult to stay in the house knowing what was going on and I went back to the care home yet again, needing some space to sort out my mixed-up head. After a while I became worried about Thomas still being in that environment so I went home to try to persuade him to come away with me and we could tell someone about all the sick things that had happened in our house.

'No, no,' he was adamant. 'Mum'll kill me if I tell.'

'That's what she used to say to me,' I said. 'But she never did.'

'Yeah, and look where it's got you!' he shouted. 'You're in care and no one believes anything you say. What have you got? At least I've got a home and a family.'

'That ain't a family.'

I threatened to tell someone about our 'family' myself and he became angry. We ended up fighting, which was something we had never done before. He was able to handle himself well by then and he did me a fair bit of damage before I realised I wasn't going to get anywhere and walked away. By the time I got back to the care home I was absolutely stewing with anger and exploded in my bedroom, smashing everything I could get my hands on. A key worker came running in and tried to calm me down but I was past listening to reason and in the end he had to restrain me forcibly. I put up a fight, my anger making me strong, and I managed to escape from him, running downstairs, swearing and shouting all the way, slamming the doors as I went. I didn't know where I was going; I just knew I wanted to get away.

Once I got outside I could see all the other key workers sitting around in their room, having a meeting. They looked so smug and so useless, sitting there behind the picture window, deciding all our fates but having no idea what it actually felt like to be us. I picked up a brick and hurled it through the glass with all my strength, hitting one of them on the shoulder. Then I turned and ran as fast as I could, still with no idea where I was going, just wanting to get away from everyone and everything. Worried that I was going to do something really stupid the staff at the home called the police out to bring me back, although I don't know why they bothered.

By about five o'clock I was back in the home and the window had been boarded up. The man in charge of all the homes in the area called me into the office. He looked like someone who had finally had all he could take.

'You,' he said, 'pack your bags and get out. And don't come back.'

'I ain't got nowhere to go,' I spat.

'Go back to your mother. You've got a home to go to.'

'You don't understand …'

'You're not coming back in here. You're sixteen now so we've got no duty of care to you.' My birthday had passed unnoticed just a few weeks before.

'So can I have my pocket money?'

'No, you can't.'

That evening I found myself outside on the doorstep, with my rucksack thrown after me. I knew Mum and the others had gone away that afternoon to stay in a caravan for a few days and that the house was empty, so I went back and slept in the garden shed for the night. It was cold and I had trouble getting to sleep, which gave me plenty of time to think over my position and what I really wanted to do.

I knew there was no point in staying at home any longer. I had tried and tried to get on with Mum and the others and it was never going to work. I had even fallen out with Thomas now. I knew that if I wanted to make anything of my life at all I had to make a new start somewhere else, somewhere Mum wouldn't be able to find me to persuade me to go back. But where? And how?

The next morning I broke into the house and went through it collecting every bit of small change I could scrounge, as well as all the food and clothing I could find in the cupboards. As I went I left a trail of devastation through all the neat, shiny rooms, smashing everything that came within reach. I turned Larry and Barry's room upside down. I was releasing some of my pent-up anger and deliberately making it impossible ever to return, burning the last of my bridges. Mum would know that I had done this to her precious house and if she ever got her hands on me she would beat me up again. Maybe next time she would actually kill me, as she had threatened she would do so many times before.

Like tens of thousands of young people before me I decided to head for London, a city that would be big enough for me to disappear in and where Mum would never be able to find me, even if she wanted to. I had virtually no money in my pocket, no friends or even acquaintances anywhere that I could turn to, but I still thought the capital city would be my best bet for survival. Once I had done all the damage I could to the rooms, I walked out of the house for the last time. I knew it was going to be tough. I'd heard that the place the homeless kids went to was Charing Cross, but I had no idea beyond that of what might happen in my search for a new life.

As I stood by the roadside with my thumb out, I felt this great burst of happiness. I was free at last. No more living in fear of Mum's temper. I could do whatever I wanted with my life. I didn't yet know what that would be but I knew there was a world out there a lot better than the one I'd experienced so far. The emotion that filled me was an unfamiliar one. I'd never really thought about the future much – just about getting through one day at a time. Now, for the first time, I felt a strong sense of hope, and it was an amazing feeling.

Epilogue

I had a hard time finding my feet in London and there were moments when I thought I wasn't going to make it, but I suppose there must be a strong core in me somewhere. I'd survived three years of solitary confinement in a cellar, starvation, beatings, rapes and all kinds of abuse, and then almost four years servicing clients in Uncle Douglas's revolting porn factory. If you can survive that, I reckon you can survive virtually anything.

Whenever I read in the papers about some celebrity or other being taken to court for 'downloading images of child abuse' or about yet another 'paedophile ring' being exposed by the police, or a ringleader being tracked down and arrested in some deceptively ordinary-looking house somewhere, I think about how little the average person understands that kind of world. What happens to some of the most abused children in our society is much darker and more disturbing than the common misperceptions most of us carry around. Children in Western countries are very seldom snatched from the streets by strangers. (It is a different story in other parts of the world where poverty is more intense and the trafficking of vulnerable people is more widespread.) When it does happen and a child vanishes on the way to the local shops or, worse still, from the safety of their own home, it is headline news for weeks or months on end, but this is partly because of the rarity of such events.

When we read about the children who are filmed being abused and the images being sold over the Internet, we are all naturally terrified that such a fate could befall someone in our own families. But in most cases our fears are unfounded because the children who appear in those films, that are downloaded by people who are unable to overcome their curiosity or their own urges to watch scenes of torture and inhumanity, have nearly always been introduced to that world by their parents or by guardians or by someone else in their close family. They have usually been 'sold' and dehumanised just as surely and cold-bloodedly as any other slaves in history. The abusers of children like me never see us as human beings, never consider our feelings, never ask us about ourselves, never even use our names. I wish the press and social services and the police would get their heads round this and learn to listen and be patient when children seem disturbed but can't explain why.

I never saw my mother again after the day I left Norwich, or Larry or Barry, or my sister. I never heard again from Wally or Marie or Aunt Melissa, and I only see Thomas occasionally. For a long time, I didn't want to look backwards in my life; I just wanted to move on. Then, when I was twenty-five, the most incredible thing happened. I met a girl who was beautiful and kind and what was amazing was that she seemed to like me as well. She must have done, because she agreed to marry me and we've been together ever since.

I hadn't thought I'd ever be able to have a normal relationship after everything I'd been through. We had problems in the early days as I struggled with my hang-ups from the past, but she stuck by me and became my true soulmate. I plucked up the courage to tell her, bit by bit, what had happened to me, and she was horrified and sickened by it, but it helped her to understand me more and together we got through our problems. We talked at length about whether I should go to the police and press charges. It would have been good to see Uncle Douglas and Joe and all the members of his paedophile ring sent to jail, but I didn't do it. I still had my strong distrust of the police and people in positions of authority. They'd never believed me in the past, so why would they do so now?

My wife and I have five children now, and I've worked hard at being the kind of parent I wish I had had – the kind I think my Dad would have been if he'd lived. You hear about some men who come from backgrounds like mine becoming psychopaths when they're older because they're so full of anger, but I went in the opposite direction. I just made up my mind that I was going to be the best parent and the best husband I could possibly be. It still feels like a miracle, but I've got a very happy, tight-knit family – something I never ever thought would happen.

Now I've found happiness in my family life, it's given me the strength to tell my story in this book. I know it's not an easy read, but I hope it will help those of you who have made it to this last page understand the evil that still exists in our society. The more people who understand, the more chance there is of getting help for any other child who finds himself in a similar position in future.

website: www.crysilenttears.co.uk
email: joe@crysilenttears.co.uk